DARK PSYCHOLOGY

Learn How to Strategically Plant Yourself in Anyone's Mind without Arousing Suspicion

Henry Wood

© COPYRIGHT 2020 BY Henry Wood

ALL RIGHTS RESERVED.

This document is geared towards providing exact and reliable information with regards to the topic and issue covered. The publication is sold with the idea that the publisher is not required to render accounting, officially permitted, or otherwise, qualified services. If advice is necessary, legal or professional, a practiced individual in the profession should be ordered.

- From a Declaration of Principles which was accepted and approved equally by a Committee of the American Bar Association and a Committee of Publishers and Associations.

In no way is it legal to reproduce, duplicate, or transmit any part of this document in either electronic means or in printed format. Recording of this publication is strictly prohibited and any storage of this document is not allowed unless with written permission from the publisher. All rights reserved.

The information provided herein is stated to be truthful and consistent, in that any liability, in terms of inattention or otherwise, by any usage or abuse of any policies, processes, or directions contained within is the solitary and utter responsibility of the recipient reader. Under no circumstances will any legal responsibility or blame be held against the publisher for any reparation, damages, or monetary loss due to the information herein, either directly or indirectly.

Respective authors own all copyrights not held by the publisher.

The information herein is offered for informational purposes solely and is universal as so. The presentation of the information is without contract or any type of guarantee assurance.

The trademarks that are used are without any consent, and the publication of the trademark is without permission or backing by the trademark owner. All trademarks and brands within this book are for clarifying purposes only and are the owned by the owners themselves, not affiliated with this document.

TABLE OF CONTENTS

INTRODUCTION 9
CHAPTER 1: WHAT'S DARK
PSYCHOLOGY? 12
   The relationship between your personality
   and career.. 13
   What are the eleven dark personality traits?........ 14
   Are the dark personality traits "curable"?............ 20
   Two ways to discover your dark side 21
   The two ways to discover your dark side 24
CHAPTER 2: THE DARK SIDE OF
LAUGHTER... 27
   THE SAD CLOWN SYNDROME 28
   The comics who were depressed (without
   your knowing) 28
   Personality disorders as a source of humor? 32
   6 SIGNS TO LOCATE A FAKE PERSON....... 36
CHAPTER 3: THE ART OF PERSUASION 40
   Characteristics of the persuasive person............. 43
   The five fundamental principles to master the
   art of persuasion. 45
   The art of persuading with respect and
   wisdom 48
   PERSUASION METHODS 53
   Relationship... 58
CHAPTER 4: MANIPULATIVE PEOPLE
HAVE THESE 5 TRAITS IN COMMON............. 60
   Manipulative men, and their vices....................... 60
CHAPTER 5: PATHOS, ETHOS AND
LOGOS: THE RHETORIC OF ARISTOTLE 68
   What are Ethos, Pathos, and Logos? 71

CHAPTER 6: NLP (NEURO-LINGUISTIC PROGRAMMING) ... 77
- The linguistic metamodel of NLP ... 79
- Operational presuppositions or NLP paradigms ... 82
- Uses of NLP ... 85
- Verbal and non-verbal skills to obtain high-quality information. ... 89
- The 10 NLPs (Neuro-linguistic Programming) ... 91

CHAPTER 7: VERBAL VS. NON-VERBAL COMMUNICATION ... 95
- What is verbal communication? ... 95
- What is non-verbal communication? ... 97
- Differences between verbal and non-verbal communication ... 99

CHAPTER 8: 3 NLP TOOLS YOU SHOULD KNOW ... 104

CHAPTER 9: BODY LANGUAGE ... 107
- The keys to body language ... 108
- The superpowers of body language ... 119
- Deception Spectrum ... 121

CHAPTER 10: DEFINITION OF HYPNOSIS ... 125
- The five most popular types of hypnosis ... 128
- Myths of Hypnosis ... 132
- What is Hypnotherapy? ... 136
- Which occurs in a session of hypnotherapy? ... 137

CHAPTER 11: WHAT IS BRAINWASHING? ... 141
- Brainwashing examples ... 141
- Intended social influence or persuasion ... 145

CHAPTER 12: SOCIAL INFLUENCE ... 146
- Cialdini's experiments ... 147
- Forms of social influence ... 151

The role of emotions 155
CHAPTER 13: THE 4 PERSONALITY TYPES 156
   A still-controversial concept in psychology 157
   Personality changes throughout life 159
CHAPTER 14: THE SECRETS OF
SUBLIMINAL PSYCHOLOGY 160
   Subliminal positive affirmations 161
   Subliminal Persuasion 162
   Subliminal Psychology in An Intimate
   Relationship 165
CHAPTER 15: HOW TO USE DARK
PSYCHOLOGY IN SEDUCTION 169
CHAPTER 16: GAMES THEORY 171
CONCLUSION 173

INTRODUCTION

The term 'Dark Psychology' refers to a group of three personality traits: narcissism, Machiavellianism, and psychopathy. All three characters are associated with an insensitive-manipulative relationship style.

Factor analysis shows that among the Big Five, poor tolerance correlates most strongly with Dark Psychology, while neuroticism's lack of conscientiousness is associated with Machiavellianism and psychopathy.

The use of the word "dark" implies that people who score high on these traits have malicious qualities.

Narcissism is characterized by pride, self-centeredness, grandiosity, and a lack of empathy.

Machiavellianism is characterized by the tendency to exploit and manipulate others, a disregard for moral ideas, and a focus on self-interest and deception.

Psychopathy is characterized by anti-social behavior, selfishness, numbness, impulsiveness, and mercilessness.

According to studies, some women were attracted to men with psychopathic, Machiavellian or narcissistic features, and others were not. Their characteristics ranged from 'aggressive' and 'less cheerful' to psychopathic tendencies, 'dishonest' for Machiavellian, and 'masculine' and 'dominant' for narcissistic.

The scientists checked whether women with preferences for the personality traits of the dark triad in the faces of men were related to reproductive success. Previous studies had found that of the three dark triad features, narcissism was linked to physical and mental health in men as well as social progress.

"We were able to show that women's preference for narcissism was most linked to their reproductive success, and we found that women with a preference for 'narcissistic' faces had had more children."

Women with a clear preference for Machiavellian male faces registered less offspring with little interest in this trait than participants of the same generation.

For women with a preference for men with 'psychopathic' faces, there was no relation to the current number of offspring.

Psychologists call the combination of narcissism, Machiavellianism, and psychopathy the "dark triad." Anyone who embodies them gets through life very well, mainly because nobody stops them.

Psychopathy is the darkest of the three facets. Those who achieve high values here are cold-hearted, impulsive, and fearless. This makes the psychopath particularly risk conscious. He is not afraid of consequences, and remorse is foreign to him.

What the three characteristics have in common is their low social tolerance, which is shown by ruthlessness and a tendency to deceive others, as well as an unwillingness to abide by rules or moral principles.

CHAPTER 1

WHAT'S DARK PSYCHOLOGY?

The personality of a person is so complex that you can never grasp it 100 percent, neither with other people nor with yourself. Some traits are innate, others acquired in education, and still, others have developed or have been lost in the course of life. Man is in a constant change, and his personality is not set in stone. Nevertheless, there are fundamental personality traits in every person, which shape their character in their unique constellation and only change in the rarest of cases—for example, through strokes of fate or long-term therapy:

A helpful and empathic person does not suddenly become emotionally cold and a manipulative exploiter.

A narcissist does not suddenly develop healthy self-confidence and a high degree of empathy for his social environment.

A self-actor does not suddenly wake up one morning as a humble and shy person.

People can slip into different roles or work on themselves in terms of personality development. But such fundamental personality traits cannot be changed—at least not easily, not quickly and often not without external help. It is, therefore, exhilarating to go into self-reflection and to explore your personality traits. At the latest, when you next sit in front of your application documents or prepare for an interview, you will be forced to do so anyway. It is not without reason that almost all HR managers finally ask about your strengths and weaknesses.

The relationship between your personality and career

The dark personality traits are not small weaknesses like "I just can't resist chocolate," but are eleven of the essential and hardly changeable personality traits that have adverse effects—especially in professional life. A study found that a strong manifestation of one of these weaknesses or a corresponding combination of the eleven dark personality traits always became a hindrance to careers over time, regardless of how successful they were at the beginning. This means that you can be successful despite these dark personality traits, but never in the long run.

On the other hand, you must not have certain dark personality traits or weaknesses. But if you do, you should work quickly to get rid of them or at least to soften them. Your personality is, therefore, the fundamental factor that decides whether you succeed or fail in your professional life. Accordingly, you should not only focus on your strengths in your personal development but also work on your weaknesses.

What are the eleven dark personality traits?

In their study, Joyce and Robert Hogan exposed 11 personality traits that are incredibly harmful to your career. Take an honest look at the descriptions below and ask yourself whether you can find these weaknesses. But please do not be alarmed: everyone will find themselves in one or more of these dark personality traits. As already mentioned, the human personality is extremely complex. This does not mean that you are doomed to failure. This is only the case if there is a correspondingly strong expression or if these personality traits are combined in a toxic way. So, if you notice a weak expression in yourself, it is completely normal.

1. Wicked

While many of the other dark personality traits may sound neutral or even positive at first glance, the case with the malicious character type is clear. They are risk-taking people who like to test their limits and those of their social environment and are always looking for the next "kick." They are ruthless and not very empathetic. The malicious personality trait is particularly pronounced in disorders such as narcissism or psychopathy.

Wicked people love the risk and can often appear charming and extremely convincing, for example, due to narcissistic features. As a result, they quickly climb the career ladder and are incredibly successful at the start of their careers.

Only with time does their impulsive and manipulative nature put a spanner in the works. They get more and more into interpersonal conflicts, get caught up in a lie, or take too significant a risk and fail.

2. Resourceful

While a tangible disorder often accompanies a malicious personality trait, its career damage is apparent. But what about the other ten? At first glance, ingenuity sounds anything but bad. It is the ability to think creatively and "differently" than maybe your colleagues or superiors. As visionaries, people who have this dark personality trait are predestined for independence.

In the long run, however, the personality trait makes one too jumpy to work consistently on a goal or in a job. Sometimes the ideas get so crazy that they are interesting but merely unrealistic. As important as visionaries are for a company, they are mostly not suitable as managers. In the wrong environment without appropriate support, the career of these people comes to a halt sooner or later.

3. Excitable

People with a robust, sensitive personality trait are less choleric than constantly dissatisfied whining. They get excited quickly and then float in the highest spheres of happiness, but unfortunately, this condition never lasts long. Instead, they move in constant discontent most of the time. This is going through, for example:

- Mood swings
- Emotional instability
- Too high demands

They are difficult to please and quickly get on the nerves of their professional environment. When excitable people are in their enthusiastic phase, they can sweep away, inspire, and motivate those around them. These would be the perfect qualities for a manager. Unfortunately, their volatility knows how to prevent this hierarchical rise as well as their regular outbursts of anger or nagging, which increasingly cause interpersonal conflicts.

4. Colorful

The colorful personality type is, of course, to be understood metaphorically. A "colorful" trait describes a very striking personality. She is extravagant, likes to be the center of attention, and therefore always attracts attention. Unfortunately, she is accordingly self-centered and tends to drama always. Thus, "colorful" employees in the company are welcome entertainers to loosen up the dreary day-to-day work or to bring a little zest to the team, but their social skills are not sufficient for a steep career. Because of their self-centeredness, they tend to interrupt their counterparts and act with little empathy.

5. Obedient

People with the obedient personality trait avoid any conflict and would, therefore, do everything to please their counterpart—for example, the manager. They are dutiful, disciplined, and in need of harmony. Their loyalty and diligence make these people the "perfect" employees. Unfortunately, because of their fear of mistakes, they are unable to act and work independently. They cannot deal with conflicts that are unfortunately unavoidable in companies, and their submissive nature makes them unsuitable for management.

6. Leisurely

The leisurely personality type is described in English as "Leisurely," which refers to the term "leisure time." It is a personality trait that presents itself cooperatively and socially in professional life but places more value on leisure time than the job. As soon as work and private life get in the way, people with a pronounced leisurely personality tend to be stubborn and irritable.

7. Conscientious

The conscientious person works meticulously. He quickly gets lost in detail and thereby loses a lot of valuable working time. People with an unusually careful personality trait, therefore, tend to perfection and stand in the way of their careers themselves. While they are great for high-responsibility jobs because they make very few mistakes, they would simply be too unproductive in a leadership position.

8. Suspicious

People who have very questionable traits have usually experienced many disappointments in life. They try to protect themselves from further injuries through cynicism and low expectations. They are fundamentally skeptical, sensitive to any criticism which they perceive as a personal injury and have a cynical worldview—especially towards other people.

These "cynics" always expect the worst and assume that their social environment is hostile to them. Suspicious people often have a high level of empathy and sensitivity. They have a feeling for falsehoods, manipulations, or situations in which something is "lazy." They are, therefore, ideally suited for a position with a high level of responsibility, perhaps even the foundation of your own company. Unfortunately, they appear to be quarrelsome, exhausting, or simply unappealing on their social environment. And since relationships are the be-all and end-all for professional success, too much distrust is out of place here.

9. Daring

The daring personality trait means that those affected

have exaggerated self-esteem and are overly self-confident, even arrogant. On the one hand, as unappealing as it may sound, it is a career-enhancing characteristic.

However, the "daring" employee likes to take it to the extreme. He appears determined, almost know-it-all, and thereby offends his counterpart in the head. At some point, due to his seemingly unshakable self-confidence and self-portrayal, he gets on his nerves and, therefore, on the decision-makers in the company. The steep career often works at the beginning, but as soon as the big promises turn out to be empty, the hierarchical ascent usually ends suddenly.

10. Reluctant

The reserved personality trait stands in complete contrast to the daring personality. Nevertheless, this is at least as harmful to your career. Resistant characters appear shy, not natural to make decisions, and exaggeratedly cautious. It takes a long time to accept changes and adapt to them. Taking risks would be just as unthinkable for such people as making quick and flexible decisions. In the complex business world, this is an absolute poison for your career. Nevertheless, people with these personality traits can be successful in a suitable position due to their care and restraint—just not as a manager.

11. Doubtful

The dubious personality trait is closely related to the reserved one. He achieves a high degree of detachment and reserve. This has an unapproachable effect on the social environment, to the point of being arrogant or utterly "strange." In any case, people with a pronounced doubtful personality trait are complicated to assess for their counterparts. They are indifferent to the feelings of their social environment and thus appear emotionally cold. With the dubious personality type, his stoic calm, especially in stressful situations, can be a plus for his career. He gives orientation to his employees or team members and always keeps a cool head.

However, his lack of social skills will sooner or later put a spanner in the works because they are essential for a management position.

A little more sensitivity and empathy would be necessary with the doubtful personality trait to be permanently successful in the job.

Are the dark personality traits "curable"?

Given this, wouldn't it be desirable if such dark personality traits could be cured? For sure! Unfortunately, this is only possible—if at all—by the person concerned. However, some personality traits such as the daring personality stand in the way of healing. After all, it is almost impossible for people with a bold personality to go into self-criticism and realize that they need to be improved at this point. This would ultimately contradict their overconfidence. On the other hand, if you are capable of self-reflection and perceive dark personality traits, you can certainly work on them.

All in all, changing the basic personality traits is not always possible, and if so, only with a high degree of self-reflection and self-discipline. In addition, you always need time for personal development. If, on the other hand, you are already able to find yourself in one of the dark traits mentioned, you have taken an important first step in the right direction. We can only congratulate you on this. So, it is not impossible to become a permanently successful person despite a "dark personality." Unfortunately, it is not easy either.

Two ways to discover your dark side

How to make the invisible visible?

Discovering your dark side is not an easy task, mainly because the "dark side" is that part of us that, many times, we still have not accepted.

The shadow

As a child, you receive a significant amount of judgments about what is right and what is wrong about you, your behavior, or your feelings. So at a very young age, you already have a clear understanding of what is appreciated and valued by your parents, and whatnot.

For example, if your parents criticize you for crying, you learn that showing strength is recognized and accepted, but showing weakness is not. Every time you feel weak, you will give up that feeling and send it to the subconscious or shadow.

Thus, it will be created as a "bag" in which each behavior that is criticized, each thought that is despised or each emotion that is not valued, will be sent to the subconscious. You will abandon any type of relationship with the rejected part.

That subconscious could also be represented by the part of the iceberg that you don't see. But, to put it in some way, you cannot stay in the subconscious because whatever you have rejected is part of you, so your subconscious will send your rejected part to your conscience, but backward.

How about the reverse?

I explain.

Why does the other's behavior bother you?

Let's continue with the previous example. If weakness is rejected as an emotion, by adults or by society, you will also reject it, and you will not want to know anything about it.

So, two things can happen:

1. You will not be able to recognize weakness in

yourself, but you will be able to see it in others, and you will not bear it.

2. You may be able to recognize weakness in yourself, but you cannot afford it so you will deny and reject it.

And this is how you learn to project onto others those discarded parts of yourself.

Can't stand pushy people?

What if I tell you that one of these two things may be happening to you?

That you have your share of arrogance, but that you are unable to see it or, that you see it, but that you do not allow it, because there is an adverse judgment in your mind that prevents it.

Really, how bad is arrogance or weakness?

From my point of view, it will depend on the situation, the moment, the person in front of you.

Do I need to show strength always?

Can you afford weakness in certain situations?

Can you be pushy with people or situations when necessary?

The two ways to discover your dark side

I've already explained the two ways to you with an example to make it easier to understand, but let's now try to create more parts of your shadow.

To do this, I propose a small exercise:

Find those characteristics, behaviors, or feelings of other people that bother you.

The latter part, "that bother you" is essential because if you do not like these behaviors, but do not move anything inside, they may not have to do with you.

You have to look for those behaviors, emotions, or people that you do not support, that make your blood run down when you see them. The ones that do not leave you indifferent, and there, you will have a clue of something that perhaps you may be rejecting.

Once these behaviors, feelings, or qualities of these people have been located, try to look inside yourself and ask yourself the following question.

That which bothers you, have you ever experienced it in yourself?

And, if so, have you allowed yourself? Have you been able to express it?

Imagine that you have felt it, but you have not allowed it.

Now that you've seen it, could you afford it?

Could you afford to be a little weak or a little pushy?

Could you try to do it today?

Could you accept that part of you?

Integrate your shadow

When you do this exercise, you will be able to see what you have been rejecting, and it will be time to recognize it to integrate it into your consciousness.

As you already know, life is a combination of opposites: there is no night without day, darkness without light, inhalation without exhalation.

So, once you have your list made, it will be time to accept those parts you have discovered and:

1. Re-appropriate the projection: recognize that others are a mirror where you can look at yourself and see both your most positive and negative aspects.

Projection

And although this section tries to discover your dark side, you can also do the exercise to determine your most positive side, trying to make a list of people you admire the most.

Write down those behaviors, feelings, or actions that you value from these people and look for them inside you.

I am sure you will find them because one can only see what it is. And if it resonates in you, then you also possess that quality. If it was not so, you could not see it.

It is essential that you even try to find that positive aspect in yourself, to integrate it as a part of yourself.

2. If you can recognize it, but cannot afford it, the time has come to practice.

If you didn't allow yourself to be weak, give yourself small safe spaces where you can free yourself from the burden of having to "always" be strong.

Don't be afraid, because the more weakness you allow yourself, the more your strength grows.

This is how opposites work; the more you go to one side, the more ability you have to go to the other. Remember that weakness and strength are two sides of the same coin.

I assure you that once you integrate those parts into you, you feel liberated, because you no longer have to fight to avoid having certain feelings and, simply, you use them when it arises or when it is necessary.

CHAPTER 2

THE DARK SIDE OF LAUGHTER

Some Comedians were sad without anyone knowing.

What is behind the humor of some comedians? In 2014 something happened that lifted the hare and shocked half the world: Robin Williams committed suicide in his California flat, hanging himself with a belt.

Robin Williams? The actor, who dedicated himself body and soul to make us laugh and infect us with his tenderness for 63 years, killed himself on a Monday in August.

What even his wife wondered was how he could hide the pain of such magnitude in a spider web built on laughter.

Later, she revealed that Williams stopped living because he could not bear the 'Lewi body dementia' that he suffered, a neurodegenerative disease that causes slow movements, joint stiffness, and sometimes tremor, hallucinations, delusions or abnormal responses to various drugs.

He had the worst of senile dementia and Parkinson's. Also, his whole life was bipolar; he went from laughing to crying in a matter of minutes. However, Williams' case is not at all isolated; many of our favorite actors harbor an unknown inner sadness.

THE SAD CLOWN SYNDROME

A study at the University of Oxford concluded that the personality of comedians presents unusual psychological traits. If analyzed medically; many even have psychosis.

"For many comedians, humor is an escape route. They take something that worries or bothers them and joke about it to try to overcome it. The reward is laughter from the public," said therapist Amy Alpine for BBC Mundo.

And it continues, "besides, depression is the result of a chemical mechanism in the brain. When they are alone, they do not have the rush of adrenaline that they get from being on stage in front of the public. And when you lack that adrenaline, the brain is under the effect of substances causing depression. "

That is why they compensate for the lack of adrenaline with drugs (usually cocaine) to alleviate the sadness of loneliness when they have no one in front to make them laugh.

The comics who were depressed (without your knowing)

The list is almost endless, and we cannot analyze nationality by nationality because we would never end. Unfortunately, many comedians committed suicide, as did Robin: Ray Combs, Micke Dubois, Tony Hancock,

Richard Jeni, Freddie Prinze, Charles Rocket, Doodles Weaver, Drake Sather.

But we are talking not only about a reason for suicide but about the lives of many comedians who today, we all owe more than a laugh.

Williams disguised his sadness as he performed unforgettable scenes such as Mrs. Doubfire vacuuming in the living room, Peter Pan throwing colorful food with the lost children, Adrian Cronau looming "hot weather with thermomedical temperatures" in 'Good morning, Vietnam' ... Long before he was ill, he used drugs and alcohol to silence his depression and dissatisfaction with life; this led to a severe addiction from which he had to rehabilitate several times. Besides, his bipolar disorder made him go from happiness to maximum sadness in a matter of moments.

Humorists: Are sad people the ones who make us laugh?

"Laugh, clown, and everyone will applaud you (...) Laugh, clown, over your broken love!" It is the Vesti la Giubba passage from the famous opera by Leoncavallo, and one of the colossal expressions of a theme that always fascinates and gives morbid: the sad, toxic and crazy background that harlequins or, currently, monologists and humorists have.

The pain that is hidden under laughter and that, according to many, is essential to find the keys that make the public break the box. Sometimes, this grief is a perpetual condition and other times, only the button to activate the humorous feeling of life.

A year ago, the monologist and presenter, Dani Mateo, told El Mundo that he had suffered bullying as a child because of his weight. "Pranking myself helped me socialize." The world was not going well for him, and he had to open a new path with machetes and clicks.

The comedian from Almería, Paco Calavera, who is the author of one of the most lucid disquisitions on the photo-cop, says that humor is a good survival tactic in the school jungle: "I remember that as the youngest of the class, when I suddenly made them laugh a couple of times, they would relax and leave me. If someone makes you laugh, your desire to hit him will stop," he tells Yorokobu.

Calavera remembers some words from the British Ricky Gervais that support the idea of sadness as a fertile bed for laughter. "He has a theory that the good comedian has a bitter and serious view of existence, and that's why he's so good at making people laugh."

The person from Almería embodies, to a certain degree, this paradox: I laugh at fewer things than most people, that's why I look for comedy. Humor, he develops, "is not about having natural grace, it is about being a writer, having a critical view of existence, a political vision in the broadest sense of the word."

Eugenio's odyssey

The documentary Eugenio was presented, in which the slippery, broken, and addicted life of the genius of the one who knows was told. The death of his first wife devastated him. But the same day of the funeral, he traveled to Alicante for a performance. Laughter, that plug.

During a wave of success, when he went from collecting 10,000 pesetas per performance to a million and a half per gala, as reported by El Español, the boat was earthed. His life became a party, one of those sprees that hide the seed of the debacle: he fell into cocaine and chaos.

Days of home disappeared. He had bladder cancer and suffered a heart attack. The excesses. At the dawn of the new century, before he died, he confessed to his son: "I want you to know that I have done very badly. I have made a lot of money, and I have managed it fatally. I have been a bad father."

It is one of the myriad stories that contrast tragedy and humor. Madness and humor. Or misery, sadness, sickness, antisocial behavior, cruelty, and mood. They are stories that spread well.

This contrast is less surprising in the Catalan joke teller. He was the least clown of the humorists: his proposal consisted of indolence. With Eugenio, it was the other way around: the public was looking at him with a magnifying glass, trying to find in his face a splinter of laughter that would bring him a little closer to people.

There are more seductive cases. Many articles compile these stories in which mythical happy comedians end up revealing themselves, over the years, as broken characters. It's funny: we are a species that left its horns to find gold nuggets in piles of mud, but when it comes to valuing our fellows, we see the dirt within the gold more.

Cases: The silent movie star, Max Linder, when he lost his fame and contracts, plunged into an abyss, ended up drinking Veronal and injecting himself and his wife to end everything. Charles Chaplin, the teacher, the visual poet of laughter, was an unbearable man. The papers of his divorce with Lita Gray described him as "cruel and inhuman." The Spanish Fofito succumbed to alcohol and depression. It twinkled in front of the children, but under his extreme clown grimaces, there was thick pain.

What is right here? Is the connection between comedy and anxiety and trauma indissoluble? Or does it not go beyond what happens in other professions?

Personality disorders as a source of humor?

Headed research by Gordon Claridge, of the Department of Experimental Psychology at Oxford, yielded a disturbing conclusion: "The creative elements needed to produce mood are strikingly similar to those that characterize the cognitive style of people with schizophrenia or bipolar disorder.

The scientist pointed to slight distortions of schizophrenia or manic thinking that could increase expertise in associating unusual and original ideas. Mild: because people with the most pronounced disorder can hardly process the humor.

They compared the questionnaires made to comedians with others made to actors or people with non-creative work. Humorists rated higher on psychotic personality. Common behaviors emerged: disorganized thinking, feeling of failure, guilt, loneliness, significant difficulties off stage, or mood swings.

The Claridge team's results, for some reason, dovetail with these preconceptions. Either because it makes the humorists' personality and crossroads more attractive (and epic), or because they lack limits of many of them when tackling and mocking tricky topics. This pushes us to assume that they don't have both feet in place.

"It is not the first time that I have heard about the tendency to psychopathy. I am surprised by this complex analysis that is made of comedians," reflects Calavera. They are, for him, wanting to look for the B side. "I'm sure there are more psychopathic people among those who write about comedians than among the comedians themselves."

The man from Almería questions this need to analyze and lay a chair on the psyche of humorists. "I do not see studies on other trades that dare to say that they all share certain psychological traits; that thing so violent and almost offensive."

In his opinion, they are always locked into extreme categories: "Or it is said that we are all day laughing and with castanets, which is impossible, there is none that is so; or it is said that we are little less than Jack The Ripper: depressive, manic, not sociable ..."

Calavera's opinion aligns with the results of other investigations that break prejudice and draw a more prosaic and less tasty reality.

Peter McGraw, a professor at the University of Colorado and author of The Humor Code: A Global Search for What Makes Things Funny, explained his findings to Time magazine: "People think that comedians have such dark personalities, but many people have dark characters and most don't become comical. Quite simply, comedians receive a greater focus of attention."

McGraw designed an experiment to learn how humor conditioned the image that people construct of a person. Participants (humorous and not) wrote two stories, one fun and one interesting. The texts were exposed to other people, who rated the authors of the funny stories as more problematic.

It is the humorous matter itself that seems dissonant, erratic. Maybe that's why we are amused. "Humor plays with taboos. Talk about the wrong things. You have to act foolishly and disclose information that makes you laugh," the author told Times.

Surviving laughter

There is not enough scientific consensus to hold a strong position; There are only some cases that are used when you want to confirm a version of the story and others that are forgotten. But the truth is that there is a point of distinction in the way of looking and verbalizing the comedians. There is a moment in which the humorist premieres brooms of thought that others do not manage to use with the same mastery.

Each era has its ways of undermining the individual, but for all of them, humor seems to work as a strategy of liberation or release.

Miguel Gila also used humor as protection or as a flight strategy. He told it in his biography. After he was shot poorly, Gila waited for the platoon (the enemy) to leave. It was stained with the blood of others. At dawn, he fled. Later he joined other detainees and began his prison journey. In the Torrijos prison (Madrid), in the middle of the tragedy, he began to draw humorous vignettes.

It would be good to say that Gila went on stage to receive that focus of light so different from the twisted light of the firing bonfires that went up to mitigate the earthy aftertaste that would survive in her mouth since that night of her 19 years. But we don't know if it was so. Maybe he just did it because he was having fun like a kid.

6 SIGNS TO LOCATE A FAKE PERSON

How do you know if a person is genuinely what they say they are? We are going to give clear signs of personalities that, deep down, are not what they seem.

1. They smile... ALL THE TIME

Usually, a smile generates a feeling of warmth, acceptance, and empathy with others.

FAKE: There is something about his smile that makes me uncomfortable.

Did you know there are signs to spot a fake smile?

Authentic smiles are called "Duchenne."

By researcher Guillaume Duchenne

It involves the movement of the significant and minor zygomatic muscles near the mouth and the orbicularis muscle near the eyes.

Duchenne's smile is believed to be produced as an involuntary response to a genuine emotion: it is considered a genuine smile.

Fake smiles:

Open eyes. There are no crow's feet.

Lower teeth exposed (the movement of the cheeks and

lips in an authentic smile brings the lips up; discovering the lower teeth is a movement that is done voluntarily).

Without seeing the person's mouth, we can know if it is an authentic smile or not.

2. They Say Who They Are

An authentic person does not have to say who he is: he just shows it. He is aware of the importance of his image to others. However, this is not an obsession, but a natural result of his way of being and acting.

FAKE: They describe themselves; they talk about themselves at the slightest provocation; they need others to know and understand who they "are."

They have an obsessive concern about their public image: it drives them out of control to feel that someone has made them look bad in front of others in any way.

They self-validate and self-affirm recurrently.

3. Confused Compliments

It is normal to throw a flower from time to time; in fact, we have already talked about how it can help in the public image to be aware of small details in others.

FAKE: These confusing compliments can be:

Excessive: you feel that they are irrelevant, that they are superfluous either because they do not agree with the type of relationship you have with that person, for the moment in which they are made, or for the effusiveness with which they are made.

With a double message: "Oh my god, I love your apartment! It's so small and cute!" "That dress looks so good on you... very flattering in the stomach area."

4. They Are Passive-Aggressive

Confrontation is the basis for the resolution of any conflict between two parties.

FAKE: It is difficult to know what bothers them, or what they think.

These people do not conceive the concept of confrontation. Either they keep quiet about what they think, or they say it with a third party. Which brings us to the next point:

5. They Talk Behind Other's Back

We are all tempted to do it hundreds of times a day; The main difference between an authentic person and one who is not is that the first person can sustain what he says both behind his back and in front of another.

FAKE: Your speech changes if you are forced into a confrontation (which, as we said, this person will avoid at all costs).

6. Iron temper?

Some people are influential and have abilities to channel and control their emotions, so they don't explode, but that doesn't mean they aren't feeling something.

FAKE: They don't get angry, they don't go out of their way, they don't break. EYE: this usually leads to unexpected explosions in which, without their control, their true personality is revealed.

CHAPTER 3

THE ART OF PERSUASION

Persuasion is not just about discovering a person's emotional profile. You have to look for unsatisfied emotions and give them a way out. Listen to what they are concerned about and come up with solutions. Persuasion, in a sense, is also a task that involves creating a desire in others.

Whether it is about closing a deal, asking for a fee increase, motivating a sales team of 5,000 people, negotiating on an individual basis, acquiring a new company, or scrapping an outdated one, situations, contingencies or conjunctures almost always come down to relationship problems and personal treatment.

These unavoidable problems of relationship and personal treatment require, for their correct resolution, persuasive action, since the other paths involve the curtailment of the freedom of others, such as threats, coercion, the use of force, etc.

Persuasion is necessary because individuals, communities, and nations often have different interests, customs, points of view, etc. When the achievement of one person's goals is blocked by the behavior of another in pursuit of their goal, persuasion is used to convince the offender to redefine his goal or modify the means to achieve it.

Persuasion is necessary because there is resistance. To resist is to oppose a force or a body to the action or violence of another force or another body. Many physical phenomena are based on resistance, and thanks to them, we can live. Why do you resist? On the mental plane, resistance is also an inevitable phenomenon: through resistance, we create lasting impressions, impact, persuade, convince, and negotiate.

Resistance, on the psychological plane, is illustrated by the principle of "cognitive dissonance." Psychologists call "cognitive dissonance" the phenomenon by which our minds instinctively reject the possibility of containing two opposing thoughts or beliefs.

Therefore, in our human relationships, we exchange different thoughts, feelings, and hopes that resist each other. That is why all human beings exercise resistance. And when you study why you resist your-self, you understand why others resist.

And that understanding is crucial because it doesn't seem very skillful to combat resistance. As the repetition of the words themselves seems to graph it, it is like "condemning a sentence" or "shouting saying that one should not shout." Resistance must be allowed to flow, that is, it must be allowed its full expression, even allowing it to reach its limit.

The resistance is moderated with "lubricants," with "shock absorbers," listening and giving space to the other. Resistance is a thought, almost always accompanied by a feeling. By subtly changing that thought, resistance can disappear.

The First Element of Persuasion is nothing but influence. And influence begins with what matters to your potential ally. Professor Harry Overstreet, in his illustrative book *Influencing Human Behavior*, says: "Action arises from what we fundamentally desire (...) and the best advice that can be given to those who seek to be persuasive, whether in business, at home, in school or politics is this: first, to awaken in the neighbor a frank desire. Whoever can do this has the whole world with him—those who cannot walk alone along the way. Therefore, the strength of mutual exchange consists in obtaining what one wants and giving others what they need."

Persuasion is a mere intellectual exercise: How to persuade is to make the feelings and ideas that we would like them to have appear in the spirit of one or more other people. And we must always keep in mind that our actions do not only come from abstract reasons, cultural guidelines, etc. They mainly come from our desires, interests, and emotions.

"If I could describe in one sentence the art of persuasion, that phrase would be the following: persuasion is to convert people, not in our way of thinking, but in our way of feeling and believing."

People do things for emotional reasons. Therefore, persuading is also influencing the emotional attitudes of others.

Already from ancient Greece, Aristotle was concerned with finding an adequate definition of what we understood by rhetoric, defining it as "the art of discovering, in each particular case, the adequate means for persuasion." This concern remains until today when the ability to convince has become a highly desired art to obtain an excellent performance in our labor and social relations.

Currently, the ability to persuade is strongly linked to the term 'persuasion,' understood as a process aimed at modifying a person's behavior or beliefs through the use of arguments or feelings. That is why having a high trait of persuasion is considered as one of the main factors to increase the chances of convincing others of our arguments significantly.

Characteristics of the persuasive person

Persuasive people share several characteristics that, among other things, increase their ability to convince others. Among them we can highlight:

They are friendly in relation to others: they are easy-going people who are close, making interaction a pleasant moment.

They are aware of the needs and limitations of others: this fact allows them to choose interesting arguments that make their interlocutor feel understood. This is a capacity that makes them believe that if they follow their instructions, their needs will be met.

They handle non-verbal communication, theirs, and that of their interlocutor: rarely does a persuasive person not speak to you with a smile and kind gestures. At the same time, they know how to read in you your needs, emotional states, and the effects that what they are saying has on you.

They study their message, calculating exactly what information you are interested in knowing, not providing you with more or fewer details than necessary.

They are charismatic in relation to others: this aspect makes us want to be like them and therefore follow their attitudes and way of thinking.

They have credibility for the interlocutor: they are people worthy of respect and trust on the part of the people whom they convince, who think that it would be well for them to be like them.

They have authority for the listener: the way of exercising persuasion from authority is not so desirable since from here, the line between the persuasive and the coercive person is blurred. However, there are people who use the scare method to convince others, albeit from a more aggressive position.

The five fundamental principles to master the art of persuasion.

Persuasion is an art. As such, it requires effort and perseverance to master yourself. The interesting thing is that its applications in your life are practically unlimited.

It doesn't matter if you are leading a group; you are selling a project idea or trying to convince your children; the ability to persuade is essential to achieve this in all cases. If you also reach it without appearing stubborn and insistent, so much the better. Well, that will guarantee that you will persuade them again in the future.

Of course, you are trying to persuade for your own purposes ... But it is vital to understand the motivations of the other, as well as to follow these steps:

1. MAKE THE BENEFIT IMMEDIATE

People care about fast, tangible results. Don't tell them that things will improve "30% in a few weeks," tell them that they will start to see a 2% improvement daily starting today.

You are offering the same, but the immediacy of the second version will be more seductive.

2. MAKE IT PERSONAL

In addition to immediacy, people like the benefits of being self-directed, even when searching for the solution for someone else.

For example, the seller of a construction toy does not have to convince the child to own it but to convince the parents that this activity will develop their child's spatial intelligence (and keep them busy for a long time). That will make them feel like they are better parents ... And it will give them quiet time!

And when you have to persuade a group of people...

3. USE YOUR AUDIENCE'S VALUES (EVEN IF THEY DON'T HAVE THEM)

A persuasive person forgets what he needs for a moment. He even tries to go beyond what the other person needs and aim for what he wants. There is a big difference!

For example, you may need to motivate a group of colleagues to undertake a project with which they do not strongly agree. Tell them that "I know they don't exactly like this project ... (recognize the situation), but I'm sure their combined skills are ideal for completing it beyond perfection."

First, you recognize the situation, then you realize their abilities (and the need to combine them), and you appeal to their aspiration: to work as a team (a longing recurrently exploited in all kinds of fiction), beyond the simple fulfillment of duty.

4. UNDERSTAND YOUR COMPETITION

To understand is to identify, understand, and absorb at the same time. Once you know what your competitors offer, you have two options: either exploit their weaknesses by highlighting your strengths or choose a lateral route...

Domino's pizza did it when it was on the verge of bankruptcy: they were not the best pizzeria (there were at least 30 better or cheaper pizzerias in their city). So the premise they used was the simple "Your pizza in 30 minutes ... Or it's free." It was no longer the taste nor the price, just the convenience of guaranteed service.

5. BE REAL AND AUTHENTIC

You may be on the verge of acceptance, signing the contract, yes ... And to encourage it, you promise (or just speak!) more than you should. At that critical moment, it is better to sin by default than by excess. You run the risk of exaggerating the virtues of what you propose, affecting the confidence that you had developed until then.

For example, if the person covers his mouth in a reflective attitude, let the idea "cooks" alone in his mind, and in any case, invite him to ask any question he wants.

The art of persuading with respect and wisdom

There is no doubt that persuasion is an art. It seems that some are born with this gift. However, it is a myth. You too can learn how to persuade others.

It is also essential to differentiate between selling and persuading. Overcoming implies struggle and confrontation with another person. Still, if we act with respect and wisdom, we will understand that overcoming is only something that satisfies our ego and that we don't need it. It is necessary to find and have the wisdom so that our objective is not to win but to convince and persuade another person to do what we want because they want to.

Techniques to persuade

One of the tools that can be used to persuade someone is reverse psychology, a behavioral technique used by the psychiatrist and writer Viktor Frankl.

Reverse psychology is about modifying a person's behavior by telling them to do what we don't want them to do. That is, with this technique, we help ourselves from the opposite aspects with the intention that the person rejects our suggestion and does what we want.

In this way, the person will resist taking orders and end up doing what we want. Therefore, the technique works due to what is called "psychological resistance," which occurs when they tell us something that we think may be a limit to our freedom and our ability to decide.

On the other hand, researchers at Yale University, among others Hovland and McGuire, developed a study on persuasion. They concluded that for a persuasive message to change attitude and behavior, it must first change the thoughts or beliefs of the recipient of the message. This change will take place whenever the receiver receives different ideas from his, accompanied by incentives.

There are four critical elements in the persuasion process.

The effectiveness of a persuasive message will depend on them, and they are the following: the source, the content of the message, the communication channel, and the context.

How can you persuade others?

The art of persuading is a complex learning process that includes many factors such as intelligence, empathy, humor, sincerity, respect, the real will to approach positions to reach an agreement ... Therefore, we are going to comment on some of the secrets of the art of persuading with intelligence and respect.

1. Sincerity

The source of the persuasive message is related to sincerity. In other words, the source must be seen as credible and true for the message to be sincere. It is good to consider our interlocutor as an intelligent person who will know whether or not our message is sincere. You should not use testimonies or fabricated facts. If your interlocutor catches you in resignation, you and each of your messages will have lost all credibility.

2. The right time

For our message to be effective and persuasive, the choice of when we are going to communicate is essential. On the other hand, we mustn't use too many decorations so that the main message can be lost. It is also necessary to know how to manage silences and to be silent when we must be silent.

3. The experience of others

The third element is based on the importance of considering the value of other people's honest testimonies. Many companies today have achieved their success based on the testimonials and experiences of others.

What a third party or user of a company says is more credible than what that company says about itself. That is why collaborative companies based on user opinions and mutual collaboration are increasingly developed.

4. Persuade thanks to reciprocity

It is the last fundamental element of persuasion. If we

receive something, we will feel indebted to the person who gave it to us. That is why in marketing, the technique of delivering free samples is used to attract customers, or in spy movies we see in many scenes as the protagonist, to gain someone's trust, try to give him something, even if it is a stick.

But in this sense, it is necessary to take into account who the person we are dealing with is and to know what their needs are. In this way, we will create an environment of reciprocity and exchange in order to intelligently exercise persuasion.

The art of persuading is not a gift of birth. On the contrary, people who pay attention to the needs and interests of others can come to convince them with empathy and with messages and actions that encourage others to follow them, since their messages coincide with the other's goals or ambitions.

Persuasion is the social influence of beliefs, attitudes, intentions, motivations, and behaviors.

1. Persuasion is a process intended to change the attitude or behavior of a person or group towards some event, idea, object or person (s), by using words to convey information, feelings, or reasoning, or a combination of them.

2. It is the process of guiding people towards the adoption of an idea, attitude, or action through rational and symbolic meanings (although not always logical). It

is a problem-solving strategy that relies on "requests" rather than coercion. According to Aristotle's statement, "rhetoric is the art of discovering, in each particular case, the proper means of persuasion."

Have someone adopt a way of thinking or acting through the use of arguments, whether they change their thoughts and opinions into beliefs or methods of seeing life.

PERSUASION METHODS

Persuasion methods are sometimes also called persuasion tactics or persuasion strategies.

According to Robert Cialdini in his book Psychology of Persuasion, there are six weapons of influence:

Reciprocity

People tend to return a favor. Hence the persuasion of free samples in marketing and advertising. In his lectures, Cialdini often uses the example of Ethiopia who provided thousands of dollars for humanitarian aid to Mexico just after the 1985 earthquake, despite Ethiopia then suffering from severe famine and engulfed civil war. It happened since Ethiopia had reciprocally received diplomatic support from Mexico when Italy invaded it in 1937.

Commitment and consistency

On a beach in New York, the following drill was developed to verify this principle, and, in the first scenario, a radio was purposely left on a towel, and a "false thief" was asked to pass and very shamelessly carried it away. The purpose, in this case, was to establish how many people would be able to risk stopping the robbery. Only 4 out of 20 people did.

Then, a small change was made to the experiment, and the results changed dramatically; on the second stage and before the "robbery," the person who owned the radio asked the bathers around him to watch his things while he returned. In that case, the bathers, who were now under the effect of the principle of commitment and consistency, adopted an active vigilance position. The result is that 19 out of 20 people actively tried to stop the robbery.

Of course, commitment and consistency must be preceded by an initial action of response or promise, and their power is greatly increased if the agreement is given in writing. For example, if by email we say: "Last week you told us you wanted XYZ, well, it happens that here you have it!"

The social proof

People will do those things that they see other people doing. For example, in an experiment, if one or more participants look up at the sky, then the other people present will also look up to see what others have seen at the time. When this experiment was carried out, so many people looked up that they created traffic.

The authority

Individuals would continue to follow figures of authority, particularly if they are called upon to do unpleasant things. Cialdini cites events such as the early 1960s Milgram experiments and the assassination of M. Lai.

Taste

People are easily convinced by other people with whom they feel comfortable. Cialdini cites Tupperware marketing, which can now be called viral marketing. People buy more comfortably if they like the person who is selling the product. Some of the trends that favor attractive people are discussed, but generally, aesthetically pleasing people tend to use this influence on others with great results.

Shortage

The perceived shortage will generate demand. For example, those offers that claim to be available for "a limited time" thus encourage consumption.

The propaganda is also closely related to persuasion. It is the set of messages aimed at influencing the opinion or behavior of a large number of people. The information you present is not impartial but seeks to influence the audience. Although the information offered is often true, the facts are presented selectively, to encourage a particular synthesis or provoke a more emotional than rational response to the information presented. The term 'propaganda' first appeared in 1622, when Pope Gregory XV created the Sacred Congregation for the Propagation of the Faith. Originally, as today, propaganda sought to convince as many people as possible about the veracity of a set of ideas. Propaganda is as old as people.

Kurt Mortensen is another Author who also detailed very neatly how to apply tactics during persuasion. In his book The Art of Influencing Others, he classifies different persuasion strategies according to their duration over time. In this way, the control strategy based on force, fear, and threat is effective but only in the short term. On the other hand, the most lasting and sustained influence over time is that of commitment based on respect, honor, and trust.

Mortensen increases his weapons of persuasion and describes how to persuade on 12 main fundamentals:

1. The law of dissonance: People usually have a greater tendency to follow and gravitate towards people who are consistent in their behavior.

2. The law of obligation or reciprocity: When others do something for us, we feel a strong need, even pressure, to return the favor.

3. The law of connectivity: The more connected we feel with someone or feel more part of someone, or when we like or attract someone, the more persuasive we find them.

4. The law of social validation: We tend to change our perceptions, opinions, and behaviors in accordance and coherently with the norms of the group. We consider that the behavior is more correct when we see that other people have it.

5. The Law of Scarcity: Opportunities are always more valuable and exciting when they are scarce and less available.

6. The law of verbal wrapping: The more skillful a person is at using language, the more persuasive he will be. The author includes a quote from Jim Rohn that says that true persuasion comes from putting more of you into everything you say. Words have an effect. Words full of emotion have a powerful effect.

7. The law of contrast: When we are presented with two completely different alternatives in succession, in general, if the second option is very different from the first, we tend to see it even more different than it actually is.

8. The law of expectations: A person tends to make decisions based on how others expect him to act.

9. The Law of Involvement: The more you attract someone's five senses, and the more you involve them mentally and physically and create the right environment for persuasion, the more effectiveness and persuasion you will achieve.

10. The Law of Valuation: All people need and want praise, recognition, and acceptance.

11. The law of association: To maintain order in the world, our brain relates objects, gestures, and symbols to our feelings, memories, and life experiences. Masters of persuasion take advantage of association to evoke corresponding positive thoughts and feelings to the message they are trying to convey.

12. The law of balance: When persuading, you must focus your message on the emotions, while maintaining the balance between logic and feelings.

Relationship

-Based on Persuasion.

G. Richard Shell and Moussa Mario present a four-stage approach to strategic persuasion in their book The Art of Woo. They clarify that convincing requires winning over and not overcoming others. Therefore, in order to predict the reaction that others have to a suggestion, it is important to be able to see the topic from various angles.

Step 1 - Take a look at the situation.

Each phase requires an overview of the situation, priorities, and obstacles the persuader faces within the organization.

Step 2 - Face the five barriers.

Five obstacles pose the greatest risks for a successful influence encounter: relationships, credibility, communication mismatches, belief systems, interests, and needs.

Step 3 - Make your tone.

People need a compelling reason to justify a decision, yet at the same time, many of the decisions are made on the basis of intuition. This step also addresses presentation skills.

Step 4 - Secure your commitments.

In order to safeguard the long-term success of a persuasive decision, it is vital to deal with politics, both at the individual and organizational levels.

CHAPTER 4

MANIPULATIVE PEOPLE HAVE THESE 5 TRAITS IN COMMON

How can we protect ourselves from being manipulated by someone?

Surely, on some occasion, you will have met a person who has convinced you of what suits you. But in time, it turned out that what, according to them, suits you is a ring to the finger and in the end, you fall into the realization that what you are doing is not your desire.

Manipulative men, and their vices.

Such people have no qualms when they ask you to set your desires aside for the benefit of everyone. They are men who don't even thank you when they receive what they want from you.

These people also receive the name of manipulators, and sadly society is full of them. They are very likely to make you question your ability by feeling weak or inferior to others. They're reinforced by the potential they have to manipulate others' values as they draw you to their playing field, telling you that you can't do it or that you can do it in their own way because they are the ones who know how things are going.

Their strength lies in emotional exploitation (and emotional blackmail); that is, they manage your emotions, producing a feeling of guilt, completely unfounded guilt, and that gives rise to you giving in to their desires.

How are the manipulators?

So, in this way, the manipulators gain control by finding their prey reward and also in a calculated way. In this section, we will try to identify manipulative attitudes to curb them.

1. They're trained in finding other people's vulnerabilities

We all have vulnerabilities, and these are the weapons they use to manipulate you. And if you refuse to believe, there's something that makes you feel guilty, and you want to hide. The malicious individual can seek to find this out, so if the chance occurs, he will use it against you.

2. They do not stop until they achieve what they want

They have few qualms about stepping on somebody, and the result justifies the means for them. When they go to act, they don't hesitate to do what's needed to accomplish their goals; despite all this, their actions always go unnoticed because they are good actors.

3. They are insatiable

Manipulation makes them feel powerful, and, as is often

the case with power, they always want more. Their moral principles are somewhat damaged, as they are aware that they are incapable of reaching a goal by themselves, but that their manipulative capacity can provide them to reach their goal using the merits of others, behind the backs of others. Their ambition fills them, a craving that, like a drug, produces a kind of addiction.

4. They need control

The manipulator usually suffers from the so-called superiority complex; They are usually people with traits close to egocentrism and narcissism. They like to outdo themselves and outperform the previous level, looking for ever greater challenges.

Nevertheless, people who feel the need to find themselves superior to others, even perfect beings, thriving by other people's merits, denote some weakness that is clothed with the appearance of strength. But deep down, they conceal an immense fear that they are poor.

Are all handlers the same?

Because manipulation is an art, we may assume that the gift of manipulation consists of various capacities and skills, under this category, different types of manipulators can be identified.

1. The Promoter

A typical case contrary to the previous two listed. The promoter flaunts power, not just a certain aggressiveness. In this case, if you're a passive person, you're going to give in to avoid having to face that person. In this way, the manipulator achieves "ad baculum" through coercion, what he desires is the case for antisocial personalities.

2. The debunker that is

The narcissism of this type of manipulator is specially marked. It just feels good, and it is a blackbird white, it has never broken a piece. He's the indicator of things, and the only thing that matters is his law. This "complete gift" would reinforce that you're wrong if you say something, whenever he's given the opportunity. This manipulator will bring out your flaws and mock you with his sarcasm. They are people who devote themselves to judging others but usually don't look in the mirror because they don't want to compliment themselves.

3. The interpreter

This particular type is especially harmful when it comes to a group of people, whether it be work or family. He has a Machiavellian and twisted personality, and acts by extracting your words and changing their meaning, a meaning intentionally different from the message that you wanted to communicate.

With this trick, he will make you wish you had swallowed your words, that they were not appropriate, that you were over the line. Or that you did not think what you were saying was hurting someone else—metamorphosing your words in this way, communicating them to the person who best suits you and modifying their intention, so you can end up being the bad guy in the movie.

4. The victim

He never stops lamenting that something negative is happening to him and asking himself, "Why me?" He focuses more on his own suffering, hiding under victimhood his reprehensible behaviors. He's still the unhappiest, well above the rest. This kind of mental perception is also called Work syndrome.

Moreover, it leads one to believe that others exploit him. He seeks justice, and he sees himself as a victim mistreated, thereby building a debate such that you feel guilty of his suffering and how unjust life is to him. A universe that is with him. So, they typically take advantage of that speech to lower your defense and push you out of sympathy or shame to submit to what they are asking for. You'll be frustrated later because it's not what you really wanted, but by his complaining, he's already accomplished his goal.

5. The remora that is

This sort of manipulator makes use of your own ego. He's able to make you feel superior; he's less than nothing next to you, a frail and incompetent guy, and of course unable to do something while you're doing. And you're going to end up doing what he can't do.

The commiseration creates inside you, and your own power ego will compel you, unconsciously, to do what the manipulator does not want to do. In this way, yours will be the consequence of such exercise without receiving more compensation than the hollow sensation of energy, which in addition to the consequent fatigue, will later become a waste of time.

How to guard ourselves against this form of person?

As we have shown, there are various kinds of manipulators. Now, what steps can we take to keep ourselves from falling victim to their psychological games?

1. Be conscious

The first thing we have to do is become aware of the exploitation. There are inviolable and non-transferable rights, and those rights are: to be treated with dignity.

- For setting your own goals.
- To voice your opinion and to voice how you feel.

- For physically or emotionally protecting yourself.
- To say "no" without having to feel guilty.
- When you work with others and believe they are breaching your rights, understand that you might be the target of a manipulator.

2. Hold distance to safety

Keep a safe distance mentally, just as we keep a safe distance when driving, so we don't run into another car and save ourselves an accident. To stop being hunted, don't let someone enter your space or touch your spider web. Without your permission, no one can harm you.

3. You shouldn't blame them

If you answer no to all of the above questions, assume that you might be the perpetrator and not the other way around. There are many facets of nature that affect you, and you should exercise power over them. Most of the issues are not in our possession, though, so you're not to blame for what's happening around you, and if you start feeling like that, try to figure out what's happening.

Question:

- Do you think what you are asking for is fair?
- Why do I want to tell you, in your opinion?
- You ask me, or you'll tell me?

Issues such as these will lead you to consider the dishonest subject which has been deceived and is likely to be searching for someone else to dupe.

4. Grab your moment

Right before you need to think, don't respond to their demands. The manipulators also place pressure on their victims so that they don't stop fulfilling their demands. Understanding how to identify these moments is important in order not to allow the power of the moment to succumb to reason and to let others' interests pass us by.

5. Make no hesitation

Do not hesitate in your convictions and remain firm in your claims. When reading the non-verbal interactions, the manipulators are very professional because they assume, they can understand it and apply more pressure before they eventually give in.

CHAPTER 5

PATHOS, ETHOS AND LOGOS: THE RHETORIC OF ARISTOTLE

In Aristotle's rhetoric, logos is the most prominent type of rhetoric. It refers to logical reasoning, to our attempt to make use of the intellect.

When we present our arguments, whether oral or written, we try to be persuasive. Just before accepting our claims, the public must consider our point of view. That is what rhetoric is; that others adopt our point of view.

So, who better to explain rhetoric than Aristotle? Plato's student studies focused on rhetoric. For this reason, Aristotle's rhetoric consists of three categories: pathos, ethos, and logos.

In Aristotle's rhetoric, pathos, ethos, and logos are the three fundamental pillars. Today, these three categories are considered different ways of convincing an audience about a particular topic, belief, or conclusion. Let's delve into the topic below.

Aristotle's pathos

Pathos means trauma and pain. This is Aristotle's rhetoric that brings with it the power of the speaker or writer to elicit emotions and feelings in his audience. Emotion is connected with the pathos, it helps to empathize with the viewer, and it stimulates the imagination.

Essentially, pathos needs collective empathy. As used, the ideals, convictions, and knowledge of the arguer are engaged and conveyed via a narrative to the viewer. Therefore, according to studies such as those conducted by doctors Frans Derkse and Jozien Bensing, at Nijmegen University in Norway, empathy is crucial to improving not only contact but the relation between people from an emotional perspective.

The pathos is used when the claims being put forward are divisive. Because certain claims are often lacking in reasoning, the ability to empathize with the audience would be successful.

In an argument for legally banning abortion, for instance, descriptive metaphors may be used to portray babies and the promise of a new life to cause sorrow and concern on the part of the public.

The religion of Aristoteles

The second type, ethos, means morality and is derived from the word ethnos, which means spiritual and moral morality. The ethic is influenced by its reputation and audience resemblance for speakers and authors. As an authority on the subject, the speaker must be trustworthy and respected. Trustworthy information needs to be delivered accurately as well.

It is not enough to make rational reasoning for the arguments to be successful.

Ethos is especially important in generating public interest according to Aristotle's rhetoric. The message sound and style will be crucial to that.

Additionally, the character can also be affected by the prestige of the argumentation, which is independent of the message.

Talking to an audience as an individual rather than as passive characters, for example, increases the probability that people will actually listen to the arguments.

The Logos of Aristotle

Logos means word, spoken word, or explanation. Convincingly, the logos is the rational rationale behind claims by the speaker. The logos refer to every effort, logical arguments, to appeal to the intellect. Logical reasoning thus presents two forms: inductive and deductive.

Deductive logic suggests that "if A is true and B is true, then the intersection of A and B must also be valid." For instance, the logos statement of "women like oranges" will be "women like fruits" and "oranges are fruits."

Inductive reasoning often uses assumptions, but the inference is merely a belief, and because of its subjective existence may not actually be valid. For instance, the phrases "Peter likes comedy" and "This film is a comedy" may fairly infer that "Peter likes this film."

Aristotle's rhetoric

In Aristotle's rhetoric, logos was his favorite argumentative technique. However, on a day-to-day basis, everyday arguments depend more on pathos and ethos. The combination of all three is used to make rehearsals more persuasive and central to the discussion team's strategy.

The people who master them have the ability to convince others to perform a certain action or to buy a product or service. Even so, in modernity, the pathos seems to have a greater influence. Populist discourses, which seek to excite rather than provide logical arguments, seem to be catching on more easily.

The same is true for fake news. Some even lack logic, but the public accepts them given their great ability to empathize. Being aware of these three strategies of Aristotle's rhetoric can help us to better understand those messages that are only intended to persuade us through fallacies.

What are Ethos, Pathos, and Logos?

In a moment, I will tell you the meaning of ethos, pathos, and logos, and I will also give you several examples. But before starting, keep in mind that this content is considered the ideal when we talk about persuasive discourses. It is not necessary for all kinds of speeches.

That said, the reality is that the vast majority of speeches or presentations are persuasive. Often you are looking for a change in your audience either in behavior or thought, and that is precisely what persuasion means.

Ethos

Ethos refers to the credibility that you may have as a speaker or disseminator. Why should your audience believe what you say?

How would you feel if Luis Bárcenas gave you a speech about honesty and good practices?

In order to persuade your audience, the first thing you need to do is wrap yourself in an aura of credibility. If they do not see you as someone to trust, it does not matter how well structured your arguments are or how rich your non-verbal language is, since it will be very difficult for you to convince them.

Three ways to build Ethos

The first way to do this is to have an ethos built in advance of your reputation. You may be an expert in the subject you are talking about, and you have an academic title that legitimizes you or a trophy that shows you have mastered the discipline you explain.

Imagine that the last Nobel Prize winner in Economics comes to give you a talk about the future of investments in this country. Will you heed to what he says?

The third technique is born from your coherence as a speaker. Your rhetoric, your movements, and the ability to connect with the public are factors that help reinforce your Ethos.

Can you imagine a speaker who stutters, goes blank, and moves nervously around the stage?

It doesn't look good.

Pathos

Pathos refers to the ability of your words to generate emotions in the audience.

Have you ever got goosebumps when listening to a movie speech? Many actors from Russell Crowe to Chaplin have done it. And it is not only for their fantastic interpretation but for the studied text that they are able to touch the most sensitive fibers. And if you add visuals, prepare the scarves.

Appealing to emotions is one of the most powerful resources a speaker has. And one of the most difficult to master.

Three ways to build pathos

The first and most powerful is to show vulnerability.

When someone comes out to speak in front of dozens or hundreds of people and is able to open up and tell something that makes them vulnerable, they are driving on the highway that leads to the hearts of others.

The second strategy is to tell stories. Personal stories or anecdotes make us seem more human and help connect with the public.

When you count the problems, you have had to park in the center of Madrid, you stop being "the speaker" and become a normal person like the rest of the public.

The third strategy is to use metaphors. Metaphors are analogies that explain complicated concepts through simpler stories.

The bible is full of metaphors as well as our popular culture. Tales like the ugly duckling or the ant and the cicada are different ways of explaining a concept. And it is just as Jorge Bucay says: "Tales serve to put children to sleep and wake adults up."

The same thing happens with metaphors.

Logos

Logos refers to the world of logic and reasoning. It is everything that reinforces your message from the prism of reason.

Imagine that you want to talk about how pollution damages our lives.

You could give percentages of pollution in different cities, show graphics, and you could define what is considered pollution: car smoke, some toxic waste, depending on which gases in the industry, etc.

With this, you would be able to give a solid base to your speech and appeal to the analytical part of your audience.

Three ways to build logos

The first is to include graphics or statistics in your speech.

When someone sees a graph that demonstrates a trend or a statistic that supports a statement, their left brain is activated and approves of what you are saying.

The second is to use research, studies, or experiments that address the topic you are dealing with from a scientific perspective. The scientific method has brought many advances in society and is, to this day, the test that all reasoning or theory must pass in order for the majority of the population to adopt it as true.

The third is to show demonstrable facts. I can say that two plus two is four to exemplify a concept, and with it, I use the logic of a demonstrable fact for the entire audience.

You could also say that FC Barcelona was founded in 1899 or that Real Madrid has 11 European cups.

Data, demonstrable facts. Logos.

Ethos, pathos, and logos: all in one

One of my favorite speeches is the one that Robert Kennedy gave in 1968 warning of the danger of measuring the progress and well-being of a nation by its Gross Domestic Product.

CHAPTER 6

NLP (NEURO-LINGUISTIC PROGRAMMING)

Neurolinguistic Programming is a discipline that tries to explain how our brain works and defines its mental patterns. It facilitates our knowledge of ourselves and allows us to change them using certain techniques with the aim of optimizing our communication capacity.

By learning how we process information, we can discover our patterns and change them with certain specific techniques, such as visualization, reframing, timeline, history change, etc.

Through Neurolinguistic Programming (NLP), we become aware of language and the importance of its proper use. It gives us the key to communicate effectively in our personal relationships, and it also helps us break our limitations and achieve profound and lasting changes in us.

What is Neurolinguistic Programming

Neurolinguistic Programming (NLP) is a dynamic model that tries to explain how the human brain works and how we process the information that comes to us from the world around us. With neurolinguistic programming, we discover how the human being communicates with himself and with his environment.

In this way, by learning how we process information, we can discover our patterns and change them with certain specific techniques, such as visualization, reframing, timeline, history change, etc.

NLP origins

It was developed by Richard Bandler (computer scientist and psychotherapist) and John Grinder (university professor of linguistics) in the 1970s at the University of Santa Cruz in California.

They wondered why there were teachers that had a full class and that their students loved attending, while others, with the same level of knowledge, did not transmit and did not achieve such success in attendance. To find out the reason for this situation, they began to "model" people who were "excellent" in their profession. Extraordinary communicators and therapists, such as Virginia Satir, a pioneer in Family Systemic Therapy; Milton Erickson, creator of Ericksonian hypnosis, a pioneer in Clinical Hypnosis; Fritz Perls, Creator of Gestalt Therapy and Gregory Bateson, anthropologist and pioneer in social and verbal sciences.

Through this research, they began to systematize similar mental patterns and identified, in that group of people, patterns of excellence so that they could be used by anyone else and thus obtain similar results.

This discipline was called Neurolinguistic Programming for the following reasons:

Programming: for mathematics and cybernetics, because we are programmed by our memories and learning, by our experiences and beliefs. We have mental programs and behavior patterns.

Neuro: by neurology, because we can deactivate these programs executed by neural networks and activate other more positive programs.

Linguistics: due to the importance of the use of language and its linguistic metamodels (a system of questions that allow for a deeper understanding of the person and their patterns).

They used the modeling technique—observation and systematization of processes—to recreate these specific successful behaviors. They systematized the patterns so that anyone can learn them and reach similar successful results.

The linguistic metamodel of NLP

Bandler and Grinder wrote the first NLP book in 1975 "The Structure of Magic," in which they developed their theory of the aforementioned Language Metamodel (a series of basic syntactic patterns that identify expressions of verbal communication that can limit our reality).

This metamodel, also called precision model, which will allow us, through language, to deepen the knowledge of the person and their mental map, consists of 12 patterns that are divided into three categories:

- Omissions.
- Distortions.
- Information generalizations.

Omissions

We are selective; we pay attention to some of the information, and we discard another part that we think is not important.

Distortions

We understand the information according to our own map, and many times we change it and misunderstand it.

Generalizations

We draw general conclusions based on previous experiences to understand reality. They are the basis of the basic learning processes.

Representational systems

From the perspective of Neurolinguistic Programming, there are three ways of perceiving the world and processing information, which are called representation systems. These are:

Visual: corresponds to people who pay special attention to visual details and, therefore, their memories take the form of images. They need the visual contact of their interlocutor, and since their thoughts emerge in the form of images, they tend to speak quickly and frequently, jumping quickly from the topic. (Circular system).

Auditory: In this case, hearing people tend to remember words and sound better, so their own language is influenced by auditory terms. (Linear system).

Kinesthetic: this system is used by people whose memories come from sensations (body, taste, smell, touch, ...) and, therefore, use physical contact a lot. In this case, as in the previous ones, his own language is influenced by terms that represent sensations. (Network system).

Although we usually use all the senses when processing information, we have a preferential representational system, that is, we think using, to a greater extent, one of the three previous systems. This is the basis of our World Map and our communication.

When we understand what representational system another person is using, we will be able to communicate better and adapt to their language (verbal and non-verbal) to make everything easier and more fluid.

Operational presuppositions or NLP paradigms

NLP is based on a series of presuppositions or paradigms (beliefs) that if we take them as if they were true, they help us to optimize our reality and our relationships with others.

There are numerous presuppositions or paradigms, and depending on the author, they give more relevance to some than to others. In my opinion, the most notable are:

- The map is not the territory (that is, our model of the world, which we have created through our senses and language, corresponds to a partial and personal representation of reality).
- Mind and body are part of the same system.
- A person can communicate.
- People have two levels of communication: conscious and unconscious.
- All the information we receive passes through the five senses.
- To know the answers, it is essential to have clean and open sensory channels.
- All behavior is adaptation oriented.
- We more easily accept what is known.
- The value of your communication is found in the response you receive.
- The most flexible person has the most influence on the system.

- Rapport is the meeting of people in the same model of the world.
- All behavior has a positive intention.
- People have all the necessary resources to make any changes they want.
- If what you've done so far doesn't work, do something else.
- There are no failures or errors in communication, only results.
- Change produces change.
- If it's possible for someone, it's possible for me.
- The importance of connecting with the interlocutor: rapport

Rapport is a basic tool in the techniques that make NLP, and they have to do with generating a good feeling and connection while communicating with another person.

This technique, therefore, allows us to try to influence our interlocutor, to provoke that good connection and empathy that favors the communication process and the feeling of comfort on both sides.

To achieve this rapport, we use a multitude of aspects such as, for example, breathing, gestures and body postures, tone and speed of the voice, representational systems (visual, auditory, kinesthetic), facial expressions and movements, distance etc.

We must divide this process into two steps:

- Calibrate

- Accompany

First, we will calibrate bodily, taking special attention in:

- The breathing
- The gestures
- The postures

Define what representational system our interlocutor is using (we observe their eye movements, the characteristics of the voice, the structure of the message, the predicates, the perceptual position...).

When we already have all the data, we go to pacing:

- Corporal: direct or mirrored
- Language predicates
- We use the representational system you are using

When we match, we must do it subtly, learning to observe the micro-movements and behaviors of the person to calibrate (observe). Rapport is established when we synchronize our non-verbal and verbal language with the person in front of us. And that we want him to modify something (we have a specific objective, or the person himself has it if what we are in is, for example a Coaching session with a client). When we subtly change our language the other person also changes it, that means that the rapport has been established.

To check if the rapport is working, we can subtly change our body posture, for example, crossing our legs to the other side and checking if the person is following us.

Uses of NLP

With NLP, we can make big and lasting changes.

Today NLP is used in many techniques of personal development such as Coaching and in many areas of everyday life such as Human Resources, sales, conflict resolution, education, etc.

The name of Neuro-linguistic Programming consists of three terms:

Programming: It is a term that refers to the organization's processes of the components of a system. It refers to the established mental programs that govern our thinking and behavior, which we can program in a similar way to how a computer would be programmed to perform certain functions that interest us.

Neuro: Which comes from the Greek "Neuron" and says that all behavior is the result of a neurological process. All action or behavior is a function of the neurological activity set in motion from the information that comes to us through the senses. The interpretation that we give to said information is the one that shapes our perception of the world around us.

Linguistics: This is derived from the Latin "Lingua" and indicates that the neurological process is represented, ordered, sequenced, and transmitted through communication based on word or language. It recognizes the part that language occupies as a representation of our mental organization and our operational strategies.

NLP: The tool that facilitates the achievement of objectives.

When we talk about Neuro-linguistic Programming (NLP), everyone evokes the way a computer works: based on the data we enter and the program we work with, the machine processes, stores, and updates the information every time it is used. In our case, the data entered would be the sensory information that we continuously receive from the outside: everything we see, hear, taste, feel, etc. It is processed and stored based on the programming we have in our brain and based on that programming, we give it meaning.

When we find ourselves in a situation that resembles others previously lived, our brain compares the data that we are receiving at that moment with that stored in our memory from previous situations. And the reaction that we will have in the present will depend on the meaning that we had previously provided such data.

For example, if, as a child, your teacher gave you a hard time every time he took you to the board and your classmates laughed at you, you ended up associating public speaking with a distressing situation, and therefore, it became something to avoid. So if even a few years after the school incident, someone invites you to give a lecture, it is possible that you either reject it and therefore you have created a phobia, or you face it, previously suffering the panic that causes you to face speaking in front of an audience. This is despite the fact that there is nothing left of the child of that time in you. You may not even remember the name of the teacher, and may even have consciously forgotten that event. But your unconscious does not forget the program that one day was recorded in your mind: "Public speaking is dangerous."

However, that can be changed with NLP: This instrument allows us to become not only the one we could be if we took full advantage of our capabilities but also the one we want to be reinterpreting the information that comes from abroad. That is, giving it a different meaning than certain events that have marked us powerfully throughout our existence. NLP works with the specific sensory experience stored in the brain, and to work with it, it is necessary to find out the structure and the conditions under which that experience was processed and stored. From this knowledge, we can modify its influence on us to make it easier for us to achieve our goals.

Effective NLP therapy involves change.

The reality, as such, does not exist. Each person has his own reality, that is, human beings know reality through the interpretation that each of us makes of it.

Throughout the history of humanity, many thinkers have referred to the undoubted difference between the world and our experience of it. From the illustrious Greek philosopher Zeno to an eminent German thinker like Schopenhauer and many other privileged brains throughout the history of thought. They have each insisted that human beings do not act directly in the world, but in the representation every one of us creates of it. That personal representation will determine our way of perceiving reality and the options that we may have at our disposal.

Based on our own experiences, the place we were born, the family that corresponds to us, the behavior of the people around us, and in general the experiences we face, we draw our own conclusions about the outside world. That is, we create a MAP of reality that will be different for each person. This MAP will constitute our guide to move through life and will absolutely condition our habitual behavior, shaping our lives and our relationships.

Neurolinguistic Programming (NLP), through its techniques and tools, allows us to know our MAP and that of others so that we can modify and even expand it in order to achieve the objectives we set for ourselves. An effective therapy implies, in some way, a change in the way in which the person represents his experience of the world.

NLP methodology: the modeling process

The methodology of NLP is modeling. Modeling consists of finding the essential components of the behavior to be reproduced, to achieve an equivalent result.

Modeling is a process that allows you to recreate successful behaviors. It is a process that consists of two phases:

The first is to carefully study the attitudes and behaviors of the subject to be modeled, to find out how he does what he does excellently.

The second is to transmit in a clear and understandable way the conclusions drawn from said observation. This is so that other people who have not participated in the observation are able, from the created model, to reproduce the original behavior that they want to learn, and obtain similar efficacy results.

To be able to model effectively, a series of specific skills are essential, such as:

Sensory acuity: It is necessary to have the senses in a position to appreciate any element; however insignificant it may seem. That is, open and trained to capture the information transmitted by the subject to be modeled.

Verbal and non-verbal skills to obtain high-quality information.

NLP is based on looking for the "how" more than the "why." The question "why" is aimed at finding out the causes that generated the problem and therefore is oriented towards the problem. Instead, the question "how" focuses on the way something is done and therefore is a generator of change. From the "how" perspective, one thing is done in one way. But it would also be possible to do it in another, making it susceptible to being modified.

A special attitude that implies being curious, placing yourself in a permanent state of resources, as well as passion and commitment to what you do, and a willingness to move towards change.

This could be summed up in three words that define the modeling process: CURIOSITY, EXPERIMENTATION, and FLEXIBILITY.

Well Bandler and Grinder, after a long time of detailed observation and after learning to model successful people, extrapolated it to people who wanted to introduce a change in their lives. They focused on discovering the process by which the person with whom they wanted to work, incorporated at a certain moment the information that caused them a certain vision of a situation. This was what later constituted their problem, (for example: "I will never have success," or "I am not able to do anything right "...). From there they set out to help him "unlearn" what had previously been recorded in his brain. And to introduce into him a "new program" that would allow him to eliminate the old automatism of behavior or thought, as well as direct him in the direction of the objective that he wished to achieve.

The 10 NLPs (Neuro-linguistic Programming)

Concepts, Premises and theoretical bases on which NLP is based.

The NLP is a collection of approaches focused on recognizing and utilizing thinking patterns that affect a person's actions as a means of improving quality and solving problems.

Among other things, NLP's goals are to correct cognitive experiences, make them more efficient, and include a set of appropriate techniques and skills for the better adaptation to certain circumstances that occur in everyday life.

It is important to note that this method is not based on any hypothesis but instead is a collection of studies, analyses, and techniques. Therefore, it is important to test how it operates through its basic foundations, that is, the NLP principles.

After setting out the goals of Neurolinguistic Programming, we present below the NLP's ten principles:

1. The map to the inside is special

One of the NLP concepts refers to the orientation people have for them in the world. The person's way of orienting has to do with his inner map. The interior map is simple in the early stages of life. The map becomes more complicated as we grow, however, and new pathways are opened.

The more complete the map, the more alternatives the individual will have for success. The map of the world is individual, and it is created from our own experiences so that each person has his map, and there are no two maps the same.

2. The best map is the one which offers more than one path

The more detailed map is also more reliable as discussed in the previous stage and will provide more opportunities to achieve a goal or solve the problem. It has to do with versatility and being able to respond to a life event in different ways. The map is not the territory it represents, but it would have a similar layout to the territory and be more useful if it is accurate.

3. Every action has goodwill

This may be one of the NLP concepts that have been discussed the most. This argument refers to the fact that intrinsically every person, and every action has a positive purpose. For example, it can be that someone believes a smoker has a good intent to smoke. Yet, according to this theory, the smoker may smoke to relax or be accepted socially. NLP helps to redirect the positive intent into a more adaptive and effective behavioral pattern for the patient.

4. The Experience structure

This theory illustrates how a certain system is composed of experience. Every thinking, feeling, memory, or experience consists of a number of elements. This implies that if each experience has a structure, its impact can be modified thanks to a change in its composition.

5. There is one solution to all problems

This idea is that there is one solution to all problems. While it will seem utopian, certain ideas cannot be applied as often. Many times, issues can occur that don't have a simple solution. It has to do with the map. The individual has fewer solutions to the particular problem as the fewer roads or alternatives he has. Additionally, the definition of the problem is related to the map material. A richer map providing more services will consider certain conditions as less troublesome.

6. All have the power they need

This is one of the NLP's principles, which has to do with the person's personal growth, as it relates to the fact that each person has the strength required to accomplish what is proposed. The problem occurs when the restricted creeds of the individual impair self-confidence.

7. The mind and body are a part of the same mechanism

This definition applies to the body and mind of the

human being. In other words, the body is influenced by every sensation and every emotion. That, in reverse, is also valid. A disease that affects the body, for example, will have psychological consequences. For NLP, therefore, it is important to change the thinking that modifies bodily problems. Did you hear about embodied cognition, by the way?

8. The importance of correspondence depends on the outcome

Clear communication guidelines need to be drawn up which do not give rise to misunderstandings, nor an opportunity for biased personal interpretations by the message recipient.

9. There are no mistakes but chances

If an individual is constantly on the move, he has various paths to attain the target. Failures must be seen as opportunities, that is, as steps that allow us to surmount and step in the direction we want.

10. If it doesn't work, you've got to try something new

People often believe that they do something that doesn't work, so they don't alter the way they behave. At this point, it makes sense to use the popular expression "do not expect different outcomes, if you still do the same thing." The NLP professionals strive to help identify and change certain counterproductive patterns that fall on the same stone over and over again.

CHAPTER 7

VERBAL VS. NON-VERBAL COMMUNICATION

Communication can vary based on how the information is passed on and how the recipient interprets it.

Communication can, therefore, be divided into two main groups: verbal and nonverbal symbols.

Visual contact is one where the meaning is verbalized, either verbally or in writing. Although non-verbal communication happens without using words, gestures, looks, body movements are used, among others.

These two forms of communication are frequently used concurrently when a message is sent, creating a mixed communication.

What is verbal communication?

It's the process of communicating with two or more people, exchanging knowledge through the word.

To clarify the meaning and offer a better understanding of what is said, verbal communication is also complemented by nonverbal communication. However, these two forms of communication can often contradict each other during the message's transmission.

Verbal communication involves using words to construct sentences that convey ideas. Such words can be conveyed either orally or by writing.

Oral communication

It is one where words are spoken or sounds are made verbally. Intonation and vocalization play a vital role in this form of communication because the message arrives quickly, and the receiver may understand it.

This style of communication uses important elements, such as para-linguistics, which, while not being verbal, helps to show emotions and feelings when speaking. So, tones and sounds are emitted which, among others, indicate fear, surprise, interest or disinterest, or mischief.

Throughout history, oral communication has developed with the roots of languages and the linguistic characteristics of each population.

Definitions of oral communication may be a peer-to-peer call, a scream of surprise, or a phone chat.

Written communication

It is achieved using written codes. In comparison to oral communication, written communication can last over time. It means that the receptor interaction is not immediately occurring.

With the advent of modern media, written communication has evolved, and will still change as science and technology continue to generate new communication networks.

Examples of writing may be hieroglyphs, notes, e-mails, or chats.

What is non-verbal communication?

This is when non-linguistic signals are used to relay messages. It is the oldest form of communication since it was the way people interacted when there was no language in existence.

Nonverbal signals may be unwittingly transmitted when interpreted involuntarily.

Nonverbal communication may become unclear because it is not always possible to regulate what is communicated with the picture or body gestures. Likewise, several times, the reader does not view these signals in the right way.

For this purpose, nonverbal communication usually seeks to reinforce the message that is verbally conveyed. And the recipient can read the message easier.

Nonverbal signals can also be conveyed via written correspondence, for example, by using colors or emoticons.

Types of nonverbal communication may be movements, words, features of the face and body, attitude, voice, physical presence, or colors.

Types of verbal and non-verbal communication.

Verbal and nonverbal communication can be conveyed in various forms and for specific purposes. Taking into account these parameters, they can be categorized according to the relationship between the sender and the recipient of the means of communication used.

Based on the sender/recipient relationship

Unilateral

Is done when the recipient does not act as a sender as well. For instance: on traffic signs or advertisements.

Bilateral

It happens when the sender may become a recipient, too. It occurs in every informal interaction.

Depending on the communication medium

Audiovisual

It includes messages which are transmitted through conventional audiovisual media such as film, radio, and television.

Printed

Such forms of written correspondence include, among others, newspapers, magazines, brochures, posters, leaflets.

Digital

Thanks to technology, digital communication is possible; this includes emails, social networks such as Facebook or Instagram, and other channels that allow large dissemination of information such as YouTube, Podcast, or Blogspot.

Traditional media now also have a multimedia presence, both audiovisual and literary.

Differences between verbal and non-verbal communication

Our ancestors hunted and lived as a group where they depended on each other to feel safe, accompanied, and to survive. Our success as a species and as individuals depends upon our ability to communicate effectively. Communication is a natural phenomenon; it is an act of interaction in which we exchange knowledge with others. There are two different types of verbal and nonverbal contact.

Verbal and non-verbal communication form our business and interpersonal relationships with others, as well as our political, personal health, and physical and psychological well-being. The first step in enhancing communication is to consider the various dimensions of verbal and nonverbal communication, and the important roles they perform in our relationships with others.

Verbal communication: characteristics

Verbal communication is one in which the sender uses words, whether spoken or written, to convey the message to the receiver. It is the most effective form of communication because the exchange of information and feedback is very fast. There is less chance of misunderstanding since communication between the parties is clear; that is, the parties are using words to express what they want to say.

Communication can be done in two ways:

- Face-to-face interaction: oral, conferences, phone calls, seminars, etc.
- In writing: letters, emails, text messages, etc.

There are two main types of communication:

Formal communication, also called official communication: it is a type of communication in which the sender follows a predefined channel to transmit the information to the receiver.

Informal communication: it is the type of communication in which the sender does not follow any predefined channel to transmit the information.

Non-verbal communication: examples and types

Non-verbal communication is based on the understanding or interpretation of each of the parts that are part of the communicative act since the transmission of messages does not occur through words but through signs. Therefore, if the recipient fully understands the message, and adequate feedback occurs, the communication will be successful. A very clear example of this type of communication is facial expression, gestures, and body position when speaking.

In many situations, it complements verbal communication to obtain a more global vision of the situation, to understand the state of people (if they are nervous, relaxed, sad...) and certain personality characteristics (if the person is shy, outgoing...). Therefore, it serves to obtain that information that the speech does not provide us. The types of non-verbal communication are as follows:

Chromium: Is the use of time in communication. For example, punctual or untimely people, speed of a speech, etc.

Proxemic: Is the distance maintained by the person with others during the communicative act. Proxemic tells us when communication is intimate, personal, social, and public.

Vowel: The volume, tone, and timbre of voice used by the sender.

Haptic: Is the use of touch in communication that expresses emotions and feelings.

Kinesia: Is the study of the person's body language:

gestures, postures, facial expressions...

Artifacts: It is the appearance of the person which shows aspects of their personality, for example, the way of dressing, jewelry, lifestyle, etc.

Verbal communication is a type of communication in which words are used to share information, whether in speech type or writing, with others. By contrast, non-verbal communication does not use words, but other modes of communication, such as body language, facial expressions, sign language, etc. are used. Here are some of the differences between verbal and nonverbal communication:

Verbal communication uses words, while non-verbal communication is based on signs.

There are fewer opportunities for confusion between the sender and receiver in verbal communication, whereas, in nonverbal communication, understanding is more difficult since language is not used.

In verbal communication, the exchange of messages is faster, which makes receiving feedback very fast. Nonverbal communication is based more on understanding, which takes time and is therefore slower.

In verbal communication, the presence of both parties in the place is not necessary, since it can also be done if the parties are in different places. On the other hand, in non-verbal communication, both parties must be there, at the time of communication.

In verbal communication, documentary evidence is maintained if the communication is formal or written. But there is no conclusive evidence of nonverbal communication.

Verbal communication fulfills the most natural human desire to speak. In the case of non-verbal communication, feelings, emotions, or personality are communicated through the acts performed by the parties in the communicative action.

It is important to comment that both types of communication complement each other, and, in many cases, they occur simultaneously.

CHAPTER 8

3 NLP TOOLS YOU SHOULD KNOW

Have you heard about NLP, but you are not very clear about how to apply it in your life or your business? Neurolinguistic Programming (NLP) has become one of the most important disciplines, especially when we want to achieve certain objectives.

This means that, when modifying our emotions, belief system, and way of communicating, we can change in the same way the reality and the image that we have of ourselves.

That is why we will show you 3 valuable tools of neurolinguistic programming, collected from the hands of experts so that they are useful to increase the well-being of your businesses and your life.

Anchors

Have you ever consciously or unconsciously suggested to yourself to change a negative sensation for a positive one? Then you have possibly applied what is known as anchoring.

Anchoring is the association between an external stimulus and positive behavior that you want to adopt. It is carried out by means of anchors such as words, perceptions, or gestures that transfer us to mental well-being.

The anchors come to act as the hinges of a door. Our environment is full of these anchors so that the brain takes advantage of them through its association mechanisms.

Reframing

Have you heard that to see things from a different point of view, you "turn the tables" or look for a new perspective on life? All these allegories and phrases belong to an NLP technique known as reframing.

It is a tool that allows us to change the frame of reference that we live to give it a different meaning, so that the emotional behavior that we initially adopted is replaced by a new one, and therefore more optimistic.

To guide us to reframing, some of the new motivational speakers motivate us to see the jar as partially filled and still not completely empty, to change the context of the picture to make it appear prettier, and to find unexplored points in situations that might seem adverse.

The swish pattern

Have you ever wanted to change behaviors that you don't like about yourself? If the answer is positive, it means that you are someone who wants to be a better person, and therefore the swish pattern technique is for you.

The swish pattern is a method of NLP that is applied to modify behaviors, which has the function of taking unwanted behaviors to transform them into desires to be someone you really want to be.

It is a tool that is helpful in changing unwanted behaviors and modes of perception.

The second projected image must produce a strong and positive stimulus, this by applying the swish effectively.

Importance of NLP tools

Perhaps what is most striking about the tools of neurolinguistic programming is that they are very effective. That is why this type of therapy is usually applied in a massive way today.

It should be noted that these three tools are not applied together in all cases. This means that everything will depend on the professional who moderates the behaviors and, on the stimulus, most related to the individual who must be moderate.

CHAPTER 9

BODY LANGUAGE

Many studies have been carried out in body language, and several hypotheses have been born, such as one where 93 percent of the contact is non-verbal.

However, body language is not a marginal impact on our social skills and an excellent indicator of our partners' real emotions.

You certainly know people who create suspicion, although not especially negative or neutral. You couldn't say what it is, but it gives you a feeling that you don't want to confess your true emotions.

This is because a contradiction exists between their verbal communication and their body language. You can even generate this contradiction yourself without knowing it!

And others radiate great charisma, on the other hand, without being particularly talkative. Your body is aligned with your language of the word, and it conveys warmth and trust.

What is body language?

Body-language is a communication process utilizing the movements and postures of the body and its expression to convey information on the feelings and thoughts of the sender.

This is typically performed on an undisclosed stage, and therefore often is a direct indication of the emotional condition of the individual. This is part of non-verbal communication, along with vocal intonation.

Body language cannot always be interpreted correctly because it can be affected by various environmental factors. The definition of a particular physical sign can never be concluded; it is necessary to look at consistent signs and to eliminate possible external causes (temperature, noise, fatigue, etc.).

The keys to body language

1. The face is the loudspeaker of emotions

Therefore, it is claimed to be a soul representation. However, as in any non-verbal language interpretation, you must be careful not to measure facial expressions individually because they typically form part of a global emotional state and can lead to various interpretations.

Is it not true that when a child sees anything he doesn't like he covers his eyes in a bid to get it out of his reality? Or do you hide after you say a lie by covering your mouth?

Though the magnitude of adults is significantly lower, we are still, to some degree, connected with this primitive behavior. And that provides a lot of hints because there is also a lot of unconscious attempts to mask what we say, hear or see in the face.

In general, it is often the product of some negative thought, such as insecurities, or distrust, when someone puts his hands on his face. Several unique examples are given here.

Covering or rubbing your mouth: If you do it, you might try to cover something. It may be an indication that someone thinks something is concealed from him as he listens.

Touching the ear: It reflects the unconscious desire to block the words. When your speaker does that during the discussion, he might want you to stop talking.

Nose touch: Might mean somebody's lying. Catecholamines, which inflame the inner tissues of the nose and can cause itching, are released when you lie. It also occurs if someone is irritated or angry.

Rubbing an eye: This is an attempt to hide what you see to avoid looking at the person to whom you are lying. Caution people who brush and rub their eyes a lot when they talk to you.

Scratching your neck: It's a sign of confusion or skepticism about what you say.

To put a finger or something to the mouth: It means insecurity or the need to calm down, in an unconscious expression of returning to the safety of the mother.

2. Head positions

Understanding the meaning of the different situations that someone can take with their heads is very important in realizing their real intentions, such as the desire to like, cooperate, or be arrogant.

Pay special attention to very exaggerated postures, because they mean that this person is doing it consciously to influence you.

Raising your head and projecting your chin forward: A sign that purports to communicate aggressiveness and power expressly.

Nodding: It is a social expression that can spread positive feelings. It communicates engagement and consent, but it can communicate that enough has been learned if it is done many times quickly.

Tilting your head: A gesture of submission by showing your throat. You will raise your interlocutor's trust in you if you do it as you nod while listening to others. For women, it was also seen as an interest in a man.

Helping up the face with your hands: The face is normally revealed to the interlocutor to be "presented." It indicates the other person's attraction.

Resting the head on the hand: It is a sign of approval if the palm is closed. This can indicate boredom or lack of interest if the palm is open.

3. Eye contact has a lot to do with the pupil's dilation or contraction that responds to the inner states.

That is why light eyes seem to be more attractive than dark eyes: because they allow for a more easily noticeable dilated response from the pupil, which is related to positive emotions.

As you talk, between 40 and 60% of the time, you usually maintain eye contact. That's how your brain tries to gain access to information (NLP postulates that you can look sideways, depending on the type of information you're searching for, although that has been clinically proven not to be true).

A lack of eye contact can be seen as nervousness or shyness in certain social settings. So just hesitating before answering saves you the time you need to access details without looking away.

If you make a case, looking squarely in the eyes is always helpful to strengthen your conviction. Yet other functions of the gaze are also available.

The size of the pupils may vary: not controllable, but with the presence of increased pupils, something positive is typically seen.

In any case, they are very subtle changes that are often obscured by low-intensity environmental changes. In the effort to synchronize body language and establish a broader link, the mirror neurons are also found to be responsible for changing our pupils' size to that of our interlocutor.

Raising your eyebrows: it is a social welcome that means a lack of apprehension and trust.

Lower your head and lookup: This is a role that transmits sensuality to men seen in the female sex. Many profile images of women shot from above (sometimes for additional purposes to display cleavage) are seen on online dating sites. For men, the reverse is true: lower shots tend to be bigger and more powerful.

Maintaining the gaze: for women, the eye contact may be a sign of the sexual desire for 2 or 3 seconds and look down. Many ways to block the view of a person who stands before you out of boredom or distrust: this is another way.

Sideways looking: a way to convey frustration, because you want to avoid routes unconsciously.

4. Smile Types

The smile is an endless source of sense and feeling. You can have a full chapter about all the advantages of the smile and what can be communicated with it. Smiling is also an extremely contagious act, thanks to mirror neurons, that can cause very positive feelings in other people.

Moreover, a vast number of smile types can be differentiated from what they communicate. For instance, the left side of the mouth appears to grow higher in a false smile since the most professional part of the brain is the right hemisphere, which mostly regulates the rest of the body.

The natural smile is the one that causes the eyes to wrinkle and raise the cheeks and the eyebrows a little.

A closed smile with clenched lips denotes that one does not want to exchange emotions with you and this is a strong sign of refusal.

The biological function of a smile is to create a social connection through the fostering of confidence and the elimination of any threat. It has also been shown that submissions are transmitted. Those who want to give up power and women who want their influence in the predominantly male professional atmosphere avoid smiling.

5. Position of the arms

The arms, along with the hands, support the majority of the movements you make. They also allow defending the most vulnerable areas of your body in situations of perceived insecurity.

The proprioception has taught us that the direction of contact between the mind and the body is mutually reciprocal. Your body expresses it unconsciously whenever you feel an emotion. The reverse happens: if you knowingly take a role, the subconscious will sense the emotion. This is especially evident when you cross your arms.

Many people think they are crossing their arms because they feel more relaxed. Yet movements appear normal if they are in line with the person's behavior, and science has shown, however comfortable a move, that crossing them can predispose to a critical attitude. Remember that you don't cross your arms when you have a nice time with friends!

That is what you express when your weapons assume a particular position: cross your arms, disagree, and deny. In a sensual sense, women typically do so when men who look too offensive or too unattractive are in front of them.

Crossing one arm in front to hold the other arm: denotes a lack of self-confidence when needing to feel hugged.

Arms crossed with thumbs-up: defensive posture, but at the same time, it wants to convey pride.

Place your hands in front of your genitalia: in people, it gives you a sense of protection when you feel sensitivity.

Confidence and fearlessness are demonstrated by exposure to weak points such as the chest, neck, and groin. In circumstances of uncertainty, it may be helpful to take the approach to try to build trust.

Usually speaking, folding your arms means fear. This is why the body must be secured. The watch can be changed, the case is put in front of the body of the bag with both hands before the arm, but they both mean the same thing.

6. Hand gestures

Hands and arms are a moving part of the body and thus provide a wide variety of non-verbal contact possibilities. The most popular one is to use them to display dominance or sexuality in some parts of the body.

They are also intended to help and reinforce verbal messages.

The brain, named the Broca region, is part of the speech cycle. However, the fact that it is triggered by moving your hands has been confirmed. It means that gesturing is directly related to expression, and it can also boost your verbal capacity when expressing yourself. Very useful for people who get stuck in public speaking!

A research found that reinforcing a sentence with gestures earlier helps the words you use to come to mind, and also that the message is much more compelling and understandable. Through this study, it was found that verbal signification, such as pointing back about the past, are the most persuasive gestures.

Below is all that is understood on the importance of hand gestures:

- **Shows open palm:** Expresses sincerity and honesty, while closing the fist shows the opposite.

- **Hands in Pockets:** This indicates patriotism and lack of interaction or circumstance participation.

- **Emphasize something with the hand:** Generally, when someone gives two points of view with the hands, the one they like best is emphasized with the dominant hand and palm up.

- **The fingers on both hands are interlaced:** Transmits a repressed, nervous, or pessimistic disposition. If your interlocutor takes that stance, split it by offering him something, so he has to keep it.

- **Fingertips together:** Communicates confidence and security, but arrogance can be mistaken. Quite useful for detecting whether opponents play poker with good hands.

- **Holding the other hand behind your back:** This is an attempt to restrain yourself;

therefore, it shows anger or an effort to mask nervousness.

- **Showing thumbs out of pockets:** In men, it represents an attempt to demonstrate confidence and authority in front of women who attract them. But it may also be a way to communicate aggressiveness in a conflictual situation.

- **Just conceal the thumbs in the pockets**: It's a pose that frames and shows the genital region, and is, therefore, a sexually open approach by men to a woman who lacks fear or sex.

- **Place your hands on your hips:** Suggests a subtly threatening stance as you want your physical presence to be increased. Many people use it for both establishing dominance in their social circle and becoming more masculine in the presence of those women who attract them. The more open the face, the more violent sub-communications it will render.

7. Leg position

In body language, the legs play an exciting role. As our rational mind is farther away from the central nervous system (the brain), it has less power over them and helps them to communicate inner emotions more openly.

The farther a portion of the body is separated from the brain, the less influence you have of what it is doing.

The human being is usually conditioned to get back to what he wants and away from what he doesn't want. How someone puts their legs will give you some of the most useful hints about nonverbal communication because it will take you to where they want to go.

The front foot: Almost always the most advanced foot points to where you want to go. It also often points to the person you find most fascinating or desirable in a social situation with many people.

If you want someone to feel like you're giving them your full attention emotionally, make sure your feet face them. Similarly, when your interlocutor points his feet to the door rather than to you, it is a pretty clear indication that he wants to end the discussion.

Crossed legs: A defensive and closed posture that safeguards the genitals. This should express women's sexual rejection of men in the form of courtship.

Getting a person sitting in a social situation with their arms and legs crossed probably means they've withdrawn from the conversation. Researchers Allan and Barbara Pease performed an experiment that found that if they listened with their arms and legs crossed, people recalled less information from a meeting.

Sitting with one leg elevated resting on the other: Typically masculine, reveals a competitive or ready to argue attitude; it would be the seated display version of the crotch.

Widely separated legs: Another masculine gesture that wants to convey dominance and territoriality.

Sitting with curled legs: In women, it usually means some shyness and introversion.

Sitting parallel with one leg on top of the other: Some scholars agree that in women, when attempting to attract attention to the legs, it can be perceived as courtship, as they are more pressed in this pose. They have a more sensual, youthful look.

It can be very helpful for you to learn to spot differences between verbal and body language. What the body shows is generally very accurate, as humans cannot monitor all the signals it emits.

Note that all of these bodily signals must be viewed in a global sense and with some limitations. Do not bring a single expression to a close. Someone could cross his arms because he's just cold, or because it's a trend that has mechanized and lost some of its real sense.

The superpowers of body language

The Little Mermaid

If superheroes, villains, and other cartoon characters

have taught us anything, it's that with our bodies, we can transmit many things.

Contrary to popular belief, we are all experts in body language, as we know how to read, use, and decode its messages. Think about if your partner transforms into the Hulk, and you put a kitty face on him to calm him down. But what very few of us do is use it consciously to enjoy its benefits. Do you want to convey security, confidence, and power? Look at 5, not at all fancy body language recommendations inspired by cartoons:

Accurate and marked movements - any movement of the body is done with security and strength; always forward.

Open posture - the arms grasped in front, behind or crossed close the communication channels and communicate insecurity. Take the posture of Darth Vader or Wonder Woman from hands to waist to show tightness and dynamism, but with authority and power.

Smile - Peter Pan, in addition to following the first two recommendations, also smiles! That gives him a halo of confidence and security in everything he does. Imitate it!

Eye contact - Have you noticed that all cartoons have particularly large eyes? This is to give them a higher capacity for expression. Use your eyes to communicate what you want and to see beyond the obvious.

Sound voice - People associate powerful voices with confidence and authority. But don't be confused, don't scream or speak loudly, just make yourself heard clearly ... like Mufasa.

But the real superpower of body language is not only in the way they will perceive us and in what we will make others feel. The universities of Harvard and Berkeley have already verified that by creating these movements, our body will also feel power, confidence, and security, affecting our behavior and making us more productive.

Deception **Spectrum**

The first step that we are going to take to know the meaning of the word deceit is to proceed to discover its etymological origin. In doing so, we will find the fact that it emanates from Latin, and more exactly from the verb "ingannare", which is equivalent to "entangle someone or make fun of him."

Deception is the action and effect of misleading (to induce someone to believe what is not, give the appearance of truth, lie, produce illusion). For example: "Mario could not bear the deception of his wife and left the city," "This financial operation has been the greatest deception to the Argentine people," "It is not magic, it is simple deception."

A deception, therefore, supposes a lack of truth in what is said, done, or thought. It is possible to link it with lies, cheating, or tricks. Some tricks try to protect the deceived (to prevent them from coming into contact with a painful reality) or provide fun (such as a joke or a magic trick).

Within personal relationships, and more precisely within romantic relationships, the most common deception is the one that hides infidelity. In this way, the infidel has sexual encounters with a third person while his official partner is unaware of this circumstance.

Inventing work meetings or professional trips are some of the tools that those who cheat on their boy or girl with another third person usually use. However, as a general rule, all this is generally discovered in the end, and most often, a breakup occurs.

Adults often trick children into developing games or keeping a fantasy. A typical deception is to spread the existence of Santa Claus as the person in charge of Christmas gifts. Parents often cheat on their children and claim that Santa Claus enters homes to drop gifts.

When a trick is to obtain a financial return, it is called a scam. This is a crime against patrimony or property: the scammer deceives the victim and makes him deliver a patrimonial asset by making him believe the existence of something non-existent. An example of a scam occurs when a person requests a cash advance as the first step in purchasing a car. The scammer claims that, with that first payment, you can start the process and buy the car.

However, the vehicle will never be delivered, and the scammer keeps that money.

We would have to emphasize that in the bullfighting world, the term deception is also used, but with a meaning that has nothing to do with those exposed so far. Specifically, in this area, that word is used to refer to the crutch that the bullfighter uses to deceive the bull in front of him.

Deception is the action and effect of deceiving someone or deceiving themselves with some situation that happens. "I don't know why I am deceiving myself by continuing this relationship." "For me, the contest is purely and simply a hoax."

On the other hand, the lack of truth that something has or directly the falsity of something is called deception.

Basically, in deception, there is a total absence of truth in what is done, thought, or said. In general, cheating is associated with tricks. Tricks, with which the purpose of losing the truth is achieved without the person being able to perceive directly and clearly.

It should be noted then that normally the person to whom the deception is directed is especially guided by the deceiver, the person who specifies the deception, to fall for a lie. Now, such an action can be done to exercise evil, or conversely, someone can be tricked into avoiding suffering with the knowledge of any situation.

On the other hand, it is common to be deceived with a humorous motivation or in those cases in which it is addressed to a child, to involve the child in a special reality or situation. One of the most common deceptions in which children participate is instilling beliefs such as the existence of Santa Claus, the Three Kings, the Pérez mouse, among others.

CHAPTER 10

DEFINITION OF HYPNOSIS

Hypnosis, which comes from a Greek term meaning "numb," refers to the state or condition generated by hypnotism. This, in turn, is a procedure that involves inducing a person to drowsiness.

For example: "The mentalist subjected a man to hypnosis and made him crow like a chicken," "I don't believe in hypnosis," "The police in the last century used to resort to hypnosis for suspects, to tell the truth in their statements."

Hypnosis is said to be a physiological condition that causes a person to be able to act unconsciously, as ordered by the hypnotist. It should be clarified, however, that the results obtained in each case depend largely on the predisposition of the individuals.

Given its questionable use in magic shows and mentalism, the general perception of hypnotism does not position it as a serious topic, much less as a science. Often considered a sub-science, there are numerous books, both instructive and historicist, that address this phenomenon that raises countless questions, even the most skeptical. Once again, these sources are not entirely reliable, given the media and sensational nature of hypnotism in society.

Differences with autosuggestion

Also known as autohypnotism, it is associated with the repetition of acts or phrases to modify the mind itself. The mechanism is to make an idea part of our unconscious, of our conception of reality. Similarities can be identified, but auto-suggestion can also be an unconscious mechanism leading to self-destruction, whether it is used to stop smoking or remove bad behaviors. We find clear examples in people who despise themselves, who do not accept their bodies, who think they are unpleasant for others, either because of their physique or their personality. These individuals tell themselves over and over that they are worthless, that they are undesirable, and end up believing their words.

Hypnosis, Therapy and Neurolinguistic Programming

Outside of circuses and theaters, hypnosis has proven to be very effective in treatments against smoking, phobias of all kinds, obesity, as well as to combat pain, stimulate attention and improve memory. Often in no more than a couple of sessions, this procedure can uproot fears and feelings of rejection that make a person's life difficult. Also, altering the perception of a physical stimulus that used to be associated with great pain, making it more bearable by the individual.

And here, we come across a very popular concept since the 1970s: NLP or Neuro-linguistic Programming. This arises from the work of Richard Bandler (computer scientist) and John Grinder (psychologist and linguist) and describes the possibility of changing the brain's perception of reality, consequently altering its reaction to different stimuli and situations. If we take into account that each person sees the world in a particular way, we understand why certain phrases are funny for some and boring for others, as well as, on a deeper level, certain images go unnoticed by some but emotionally block others.

NLP can act on trauma, causing the patient to relive memories, reinterpret them with their unfailingly more mature mind, and restore them. According to studies, it is currently impossible to erase a portion of memory. This is the only way, discovered so far, to help those people living tormented by a horrible past, which they would discard if they had the opportunity.

Also, this type of therapy achieves very positive results to reinforce self-confidence. It is often applied to patients with self-esteem problems, offering them a much more positive vision of themselves and demonstrating, or allowing them to discover, those virtues that have been relegated for years.

Theories about hypnosis

Hypnosis is the subject of a variety of separate and contradictory hypotheses, some of which concentrate on brain function and others on the nature of the condition. Furthermore, there is a clear division between those who believe that consciousness prevails during the state of hypnotism and those who deny it flatly.

The five forms of hypnosis and their operating conditions

There is no one way to hypnotize. We show you the different forms that this technique can take.

Hypnosis is a technique that facilitates behavioral changes through suggestion. Depending on the term we use, we may classify hypnosis as a psychological disorder or a sequence of mental behaviors and processes; today, it is correlated with beliefs or brain waves by the medical community.

Throughout this section, we will look at the five most popular forms of hypnosis: the standard approach centered upon direct oral instructions, cognitive-compartmental hypnosis, self-hypnosis, neurology, and programming or NLP.

The five most popular types of hypnosis

Here are 5 of the best-known methods, including the use of hypnosis. There are, of course, many other variants, and practitioners or instruments can combine more than one form.

1) **Modern hypnosis (by suggestion)**
   The origin of mainstream hypnosis goes back to the unusual methods used by Franz Mesmer in

magnets and popularized at the end of the 18th century. Earlier, James Braid expressed his resistance to the theory of the mesmeric system and proposed the hypnosis to be a nervous system condition.

The typical hypnosis is based on the induction of a trance state. When the hypnotized person enters the trance state, his actions and mental contents are indicated in verbal form. Thus, the objective of this method is to influence behavior, for example, by suggesting that the person abandon a negative habit or belief.

Today the classical method is still the most widely used form of hypnosis worldwide. It is theoretical in terms of the theory of Freud's unconscious mind, which, in addition to shaping guidelines so different from cognitivism, has characterized the later developments in psychoanalysis critically.

2) **Ericksonian hypnosis**

This form of hypnosis is a product of a pioneer in this area and psychotherapy in general, an American psychologist, Milton H. Erickson. This author shouldn't be confused with Erik Erikson, a German evolutionary psychologist who is best known for his eight-stage psychosocial theory.

Ericksonian hypnosis is not achieved by straightforward instructions, but by metaphors that encourage creativity and contemplation. Because of this, it is attributed to greater effectiveness than classic hypnosis in people who are refractory to hypnosis, with low suggestibility or who are skeptical about the procedure.

Erickson's influence is not limited to hypnosis and neurolinguistic programming, which we will discuss later. The strategic school and the quick therapy focused on approaches, both parts of the systematic approach took on the core feature of its intervention model, the weight of the interaction between the therapist and the client for achieving change.

3) Cognitive-computer hypnosis

The cognitive-computing viewpoint views hypnosis as a series of approaches that facilitate behavioral improvements through recommendations. The relationship between variables such as physical rest, the use of imagination, or the individual's desires and values is a result of this phenomenon.

Those clinicians who adhere to cognitive behavioral therapy use strategies for hypnosis to supplement broader procedures. It was extended in this context to issues as diverse as sleep-wake cycle disorders, psychiatric, drug-related disorders or post-traumatic stress disorders (in particular, tobacco).

4) Self-hypnosis

We speak of self-hypnosis when a person induces himself in this state through autosuggestion. Instruments that serve as supports are often used; the most popular are sound recordings, but tools that modify brain waves to alter the level of consciousness are also available.

This form of hypnosis is primarily used for non-particularly severe everyday difficulties. Therefore, for example, intrapersonal and interpersonal skills (such as stressfulness), stress management, and relaxation can be created, the scenario can be met, weight loss, and smoking can stop.

5) **Neurolinguistic programming (NLP)**

While it's not a hypnotic thing to say, the neural conditioning is closely related to these approaches (usually referred to as "NLP"). This method was developed for psychologically enhancing skills by Richard Bandler and John Grinder using "pension models."

The Milton Model is based on the hypnosis method developed by Milton Erickson; in this variant of NLP, the suggestion is practiced through metaphors. The use made by Bandler and Grinder in the Ericksonian hypnosis was, however, criticized for altering or underviewing many of their fundamental ideas.

Neurological programming is known by the scientific community as pseudo-science and, therefore, as a fraud. His theories do not base themselves on an empirical framework, even though it does incorporate abstract concepts to give "theory" an air of legitimacy.

Myths of Hypnosis

The myths in hypnosis come from several centuries ago, either due to misinterpretations or unfounded beliefs, and that may condition us not to grasp the fundamental concepts of the practice of hypnosis.

With this, we try to normalize the most common hypnosis myths that usually affect the understanding and acceptance of this technique as a therapeutic tool.

Myth 1: The hypnotized subject is highly suggestible and can do whatever the hypnotist instructs

The suggestion is a part of the hypnotic process, which is reached after the induction phase. This phase can be accessed in very different ways: by an object attributed to a hypnogenic power like a clock, or by a suggestive mimicry. Or, by a simple blow of effect like a clap followed by the word "dream" that causes an interruption in the hypnotizable individual and causes him to enter a trance state.

The suggestion does not even require the presence of the suggestion, as it happens in the cases of autosuggestion, or the hypnotization at a distance using a recording or using the telephone.

It is in the suggestion phase the hypnotized are given a series of "suggestions," as their name suggests, so that they do, feel or perceive what the hypnotist tells them.

But in no case can suggestion make the subject do things contrary to his ethical code or contrary to the laws of nature. You cannot get a person to fly or override the law of gravity, nor can they lift a weight for which they are not physically prepared to bear.

Most often, the suggestions influence aspects that we are not consciously able to influence, such as digestion, respiration, body temperature. And also on the mind, enhancing psychic factors such as imagination, sensory perception, or increasing memory.

They can indeed be accomplished with suggestions that a person sees where there is no or stops seeing where there is. This is what we call positive or negative hallucinations, which revert once the suggestion is annulled and are nothing more than natural phenomena of increased imagination.

We do need to differentiate between the INTRAHIPNÓTICAS SUGGESTIONS, that is, those occurring during the hypnotic trance, and the POSTHIPNÓTICAS, those occurring under an intrahepatic order, after leaving the trance and before the effect of a particular trigger.

For example: "When you wake up, you will feel very calm, and that tranquility you will take with you every day until the next session. And every time you bring a glass of water to your mouth, you will realize that you are doing something very important for yourself ... The contact of the water with your lips will remind you that every time you drink, you are bringing something very necessary to you... The fact of drinking water makes you feel that you are moving towards your desired state, feeling more and more relaxed and at ease with yourself. "

Myth 2: Hypnosis achieves little less than magical results in the hypnotized

The conviction that is also very popular is that hypnosis is quite convenient, simple, successful therapy that needs no effort on the part of the consumer to change their behavior.

Hypnosis is a technique that makes the result of an operation simpler, rather than a treatment itself. Like other ways of using suggestion, it can speed up treatment, decreasing the person's subjective effort. However, the patient must be actively involved in the treatment to obtain the desired benefits.

Hypnosis is only one of the many working tools that the psychologist or doctor can use within the therapeutic context if he sees fit. Hypnosis does not "cure" anything of its own, and no one can hypnotize what they are not prepared to do without hypnosis.

For this reason, hypnosis can only be applied with guarantees, a professional duly qualified and trained for what he intends to solve, and provided that he is expressly qualified, also, to apply the hypnotic techniques of his patients.

Myth 3: Under the hypnotic state, you can access past lives or contact deceased people

The extraordinary hypnotic phenomena, the revival of past experiences, and other unusual events that are sometimes described as occurring under a hypnotic state have not been proven by science. Before them, we must keep a certain reserve, at least.

Recalling past lives, speaking unknown languages, or other intra-hypnotic paranormal phenomena, but without dismissing the likelihood that they could have happened in certain cases, is not an easy thing to do daily. There is still much to be discovered about its origin before concluding with adequate empirical validity.

Myth 4: The person who goes into a deep trance does not remember anything later

Amnesia may indeed occur on certain occasions during the trance, either under the hypnotist's command or spontaneously.

It is not regularly occurring in any case unless you access forgotten traumatic memories and choose to leave this field inaccessible from the consciousness in the benefit of the individual.

If it is very frequent, however, a temporal distortion occurs, since the subject during the trance has the perception that much less time passes than what happens in reality.

So, when you finish the trance process, open your eyes and look at the clock. You will have the feeling that much more time has passed than you thought: this is a characteristic of the trance state.

Myth 5: The hypnotized may remain forever in a hypnotic state

One of the most widespread myths is the fear of not being able to wake up, which we discussed earlier. This is something unfounded since the only thing that can happen, and, can quickly occur, is that the hypnotized person enters a physiological dream, from which you will wake up in the same way that you wake up every morning after the night's sleep.

What is Hypnotherapy?

Hypnosis or Hypnotherapy is a type of psychotherapy that uses guided methods of relaxation and intense concentration, focusing the client's attention to achieve a high state of consciousness that is sometimes called a trance. The person's attention is so concentrated that while in this state, everything that happens around him is temporarily blocked or ignored by the person who is in the hypnotic trance. An individual with the aid of a qualified therapist can focus their attention on certain thoughts or duties in this natural state.

How does hypnosis function?

The hypnotic state helps people to examine negative thoughts, emotions, and experiences that may have been shielded from their conscious minds. As an aid for psychotherapy in general, hypnosis can be used. Hypnosis can also encourage people to perceive other things differently, such as suppressing pain perception.

Hypnosis can be used as a treatment or medical diagnosis in two ways.

The most important risk is the likelihood of having false remembrances and becoming less successful than other, more proven, conventional psychiatric therapies.

Analysis: This approach uses a state of relaxation to investigate a potential psychological root cause of disease and symptoms, including an incident of trauma that a person has unconsciously suppressed. The pain can be dealt with in psychotherapy until it is known.

Which occurs in a session of hypnotherapy?

The therapist's initial task is to establish a good relationship with the client. This involves encouraging the client to talk about their concerns. The therapist may spend time with him first to conduct a medical history. As well as establishing a medical history, the examination helps to build trust between the therapist and the client. Feeling safe and comfortable with the therapist helps induce a hypnotic trance.

The goals for therapy are discussed and agreed between the two, and a full explanation of what Hypnosis consists of is provided. Any questions or misconceptions about hypnosis are also addressed.

A trance state is possible in several different ways. The therapist talks in a quiet, gentle voice and generally sits on a chair or a recliner. You may be asked to imagine or visualize yourself walking down a path, or you may be made to look at a fixed point, or simply hear the sound of the therapist's voice. To deepen the trance, the therapist can count from 10 to 1 or ask you to imagine walking down a flight of stairs. You will then feel very relaxed, but aware of your surroundings.

The duration of treatments depends on the problem or symptoms and individual circumstances. With some people, a problem like nail-biting can be successfully treated in one sitting. Other problems, like panic attacks, can take up to 5 or 6 sessions.

During therapy, clients are taught to induce self-hypnosis as part of a series of therapeutic home tasks.

It normally takes 1 ½ hours to start the first session and then 1 ½ hours after.

Things you should know about hypnosis:

- One can still be hypnotized against their will as they always track all the feedback, even though they are hypnotized.

- The entire aim of clinical hypnosis is to restore the lost control, and hence the symptom or problem has been induced.
- Approximately 85% of people of all ages are expected to respond easily to hypnosis.

How is Hypnosis beneficial?

The hypnotic state allows an individual to have more discussion and proposals. For several illnesses, it may improve many therapies, including:

- Phobias, fears, and anxiety
- Sleep disorders
- Depression
- Stress
- Post-traumatic stress
- The pain of loss

Hypnosis can also be used to relieve discomfort and resolve problems such as smoking or unhealthy consumption. This may also be effective for those with serious symptoms who need to tackle emergencies.

What are the disadvantages of Hypnosis?

The case of a person with psychotic symptoms, such as hallucinations and delusions, or anyone who uses narcotics or alcohol, cannot be suitable for hypnosis. It can only be used to manage pain after a doctor has examined the individual for any physical condition that needs medication or surgery. Hypnosis may also be a less effective form of therapy than other psychiatric disorders.

Some therapists use Hypnosis to retrieve repressed memories, which they possibly believe are linked to a person's mental disorder. Hypnosis, however, often poses a risk of false impressions, usually as a result of the therapist's unwanted suggestions. That's why the use of hypnosis is still controversial with many mental illnesses, including dissociative disorders.

Is it risky to get hypnosis?

No negative technique is hypnosis. It is not controlling or brainwashing, as was often claimed. A therapist cannot make a person uncomfortable or unable to do something. The most significant danger is that false remembrances would be less likely than other traditional psychological therapies that have proved to be more effective.

CHAPTER 11

WHAT IS BRAINWASHING?

The concept of "brainwashing" is very close to that of "mind control." It is an idea without a strictly scientific basis. It proposes that the will, thoughts and other mental facts of individuals can be modified through persuasion techniques, with which unwanted ideas would be introduced into the psyche of a "victim."

If we define the concept in this way, we see that it bears a marked similarity with another more typical of the vocabulary of psychology: that of suggestion, which refers to the influence that some individuals can exert on the mental contents of others (or on the own, in which case we speak of autosuggestion). However, the term "suggestion" is less ambitious.

Although the idea of brainwashing is not entirely incorrect, this popular concept has unscientific connotations that have led many experts to reject it in favor of more modest ones. The instrumental use of the term in legal proceedings has contributed to this, especially in disputes over child custody.

Brainwashing examples

It is common for complex phenomena such as suicide or terrorism to be explained by many people through the concept of brainwashing, especially in cases in which the subjects are seen as young and influential people.

Something similar applies to sects, religions, conduct during wars, or radical political ideologies.

Concerning the latter case, it is worth mentioning that brainwashing has been used above all in attempts to give a simple explanation to events related to violence. Events such as the massacres that occurred in the context of Nazism and other types of totalitarianism.

Subliminal advertising is another fact that we can relate to the idea of brainwashing. This type of promotion, which is prohibited in countries like the United Kingdom, consists of the inclusion of messages that do not reach the threshold of consciousness but are automatically perceived.

Moreover, psychology itself has often been accused of being a brainwashing method. Particularly well-known is the case of Pavlov and Skinner's behaviorism, criticized by other experts and in works such as "The Clockwork Orange." Psychoanalysis and techniques such as cognitive restructuring have received similar signs of rejection.

History and popularization of the concept

The concept of brainwashing first emerged in China to describe the Chinese Communist Party's persuasion of opponents of the Maoist government. The term "xinao," which literally translates as "brainwash," was a play on words that referred to the cleansing of the mind and body promoted by Taoism.

In the 1950s, the term was adopted and applied by the United States Army and Government to justify the fact that some American prisoners had collaborated with their captors during the Korean War. It has been argued that their objective may have been to limit the public impact of the revelation that chemical weapons had been used.

Later Russian historian Daniel Romanovsky claimed that the Nazis had used brainwashing techniques (including re-education programs and mass propaganda) to promote their ideas among the population of Belarus. In particular, the conception of the Jews as an inferior race.

However, the popularization of brainwashing is primarily due to popular culture. Before "The Clockwork Orange" appeared the novel "1984" by George Orwell, in which a totalitarian government manipulates the population through lies and coercion. Sauron's mind control in "The Lord of the Rings" has also been associated with brainwashing.

View from psychology

Psychology generally understands the phenomena attributed to brainwashing through more operative and more limited concepts, such as persuasion and suggestion, which includes hypnosis. In these cases, changes in behavior depend largely on the subject's autosuggestion from external stimuli.

In 1983 the American Psychological Association, the hegemonic body in the field of psychology, commissioned clinical psychologist Margaret Singer to lead a working group to investigate the phenomenon of brainwashing. However, they accused Singer of presenting biased data and speculation, and the project was canceled.

It cannot be stated categorically that brainwashing exists as an independent phenomenon due to the ambiguity of its formulation. In any case, many authors defend that the use of powerful persuasion techniques is evident in contexts such as the media and advertising; however, it is advisable to avoid such topics.

Social influence happens when a person is influenced by feelings, beliefs or behaviors. In other ways, social power can be seen in reverence, socialization, peer pressure, loyalty, leadership, persuasion, marketing and sales. In 1958, psychologist Herbert Kelman described three different methods of shaping society.

Social influence

In the face of a persuasive message, the recipient can:

- Process the message rationally.

- Let yourself be carried away by heuristics.

For some authors such as Allport, social influence is the central object of study in Social Psychology. Allport defines the study of social influence: I try to understand and explain the way in which the thoughts, feelings, and behaviors of individuals are influenced by the real, imagined, or implicit presence of others. People intervene, sometimes as an influential agent, sometimes as a target that is influenced by other human beings. Influence is not always deliberate or explicit.

Intended social influence or persuasion

Through the processes of influence and persuasion, our affections, beliefs, attitudes, intentions, and behaviors are configured. The intention to influence is always aimed at achieving a change in the behavior of others, individuals, or groups. Sometimes the objective is to achieve a specific behavior (that they prepare breakfast for us); other times, it is intended to influence attitudes (announcement of nature). Attempts to influence can occur in face-to-face processes.

CHAPTER 12

SOCIAL INFLUENCE

Social influence occurs when emotions, opinions, or behaviors are affected by another person. Although it may seem that it is not very common, since most of the people with whom we deal are not going to try to change our attitudes, social influence occurs continuously in our lives.

From the moment we enter a supermarket, the vendors are going to offer us discounted products. The mechanic is going to advise us on a tire change when we only want to check the car oil. Friends are going to tell us which music is the best. Our partner will advise us on our wardrobe. Thus, in a large number of situations, others will try to influence us almost without us noticing.

First contributions to social influence

Social influence has been a major topic in social psychology. In the past, social influence has been used to explain acts as horrifying as those committed by the Nazis. It has also served to explain the behaviors of traitors who abandoned their side to fight with the opposite side.

To reach these conclusions, many experiments were carried out. Among them, three stand out for the revolution they supposed at the time. These experiments broke with preconceived beliefs, and their results were hardly assumable. These experiments were as follows:

Cialdini's experiments

One of the most famous researchers in this field is Robert Cialdini. Working as a car salesman, Cialdini discovered six factors of social influence that he called the "weapons of influence" (Cialdini, 2001). These factors are the following:

- **Reciprocity:** People need to return favors. Doing a favor imposes a debt, and the other person needs to pay it off. If you invite someone to dinner, this person will most likely end up paying you back.

- **Commitment and coherence:** Be and appear coherent with the declarations or with the acts previously carried out. Imagine that you are going to buy a house and the seller indicates the price. You agree and decide to buy it. A few days later, the seller tells you that the price is slightly higher since he had looked at it wrong. As you had already said yes and you had promised, for being consistent, most likely, you will accept the new price.

- **Social approval:** Feeling included. What a large number of people do tends to be considered valid. If all your friends think that a certain brand of car is the most reliable, surely your opinion will end up being the same as theirs. As the saying goes: "too much evil, the consolation of fools."

- **Authority:** The explanations given by someone who considers himself important or who comes from an institution seems more credible. Actor Hugh Laurie has been hired to make drug announcements since, despite not being a doctor, playing one (House series) has given him a similar advertising projection.

- **Sympathy:** When there is physical attraction, it is easier to convince someone of something. Sympathy and similarities are going to be key factors in persuading people. A study from the United States showed that when a woman was charged and went to trial, she received lesser penalties when she was attractive than when she was not.

- **Scarcity:** The perception of scarcity generates demand. When a product is presented as limited in time or accessibility, it leads to a change in purchasing attitude. Many stores use techniques such as offering products or prices for a limited time or offer limited units.

Foot in the door

Within the category of commitment and coherence, we find a famous technique called "the foot in the door." This technique consists of making a small request that the vast majority of people will accept, and then make a larger one, which is the real request.

In 1966 Freedman and Fraser conducted an experiment on the foot in the door. They asked several people to put up a large, ugly sign in their garden that said, "Drive carefully." Only 17% agreed. Another group of people was first asked to sign a document in favor of road safety. This petition involved little commitment, which is why almost everyone signed.

What happened? When, weeks later, they asked this second group to put the poster in their garden, 55% of the people agreed. In this way, you can see how we can be manipulated without realizing it. What we would not do at first, we would access it through a small "manipulative act."

Asch's Experiment

Another classic study in the field of social influence is that of Solomon Asch (1956). This researcher would gather groups of people in one room and show them a line drawing. He then showed them three lines of different sizes, one of which was the same length as the previously shown line and asked them to tell which line was the same length as the first line.

Everyone in the room was in the league, except one. When all the people in agreement agreed that the line of similar size was the wrong one, the participant who did not know anything about what was going on behind their back on several occasions ended up choosing the wrong line as well as the others.

This experiment was carried out with different variants, changing the number of people and the position in which the participant gave his answer. The more people opted for the wrong option before that participant, the more likely they were to choose the majority option. Also, the fact that there was one person who disagreed with the majority made it more likely that the participant chose the correct option and not the one that erroneously indicated the majority.

Milgram's experiment

Finally, another of the classic experiments in psychology is that of Stanley Milgram (1974). This researcher asked a participant to ask questions of another participant who was in a booth. Each time a question failed, the participant had to press a button that administered a shock and raise the voltage.

The participant who answered the questions and received the downloads was an actor who feigned the downloads, which were not real. Most of the participants, despite screaming in pain from the other participant, managed to deliver shocks so strong that they could lead to death. Throughout the process, the researcher told the participant that they should continue.

Subsequently, various studies showed that when people were asked what maximum discharge, they would be able to give, they prevent the authority of the researcher and tend to give low data. However, when they participate in the experiment, the researcher's voice telling them to continue is enough for them to do so.

Forms of social influence

Currently, it is considered that social influence can occur in different ways:

- **Compliance:** Compliance is the degree to which emotions, opinions, or feelings will change to fit the group's opinions. Social groups often have norms and values that indicate what to think and when. If we do not accept it, we will not enter the group. Therefore, to be members of the group we are going to change our opinions for theirs. We are going to settle for what they tell us.

- **Socialization:** Socialization consists of internalizing the norms and ideology of a society. It is a learning process that lasts a lifetime. There are a series of social agents who will transmit the socialization process to us. The most important social agents are the family and the school.

- **Peer pressure:** Peer pressure or social pressure is the influence of a group of peers. This pressure usually occurs from other people like friends and family. The strongest peer pressure may be that of adolescence.

- **Obedience:** Obedience consists of listening to order and following it. Orders can consist of actions that are performed or omitted. In obedience, there is a key figure; that of authority. This can be from a person to a community or an idea. He is a figure who, above all, deserves obedience for different reasons.

- **Leadership:** Leadership is the set of managerial skills to influence the way of being or acting of people or a workgroup. These skills are used to make the person or teamwork enthusiastically achieve their goals and objectives. These capabilities include the ability to delegate, take the initiative, manage, convene, promote, encourage, motivate, and evaluate a project, among others.

- **Persuasion:** Persuasion is a process aimed at changing the attitude or behavior of a person or a group towards some event, idea, object or person. This is done by using words to convey information, feelings, or reasoning, or a combination thereof. It is influencing someone through words. Persuasion is equated with rhetoric.

Cognitive dissonance

But why do all these methods of social influence work? Although there are various explanations, one of the theories that have gained more strength over time is the theory of cognitive dissonance (Festiger, 1957). Cognitive dissonance occurs when two thoughts conflict or when a behavior conflicts by not adapting to previous beliefs (Ex: someone who thinks that killing is bad and ends up killing, someone who thinks that smoking is bad and ends up smoking).

Cognitive dissonance is understood as the tension caused by the lack of internal harmony in the system of ideas, beliefs, and emotions. When two ideas or behaviors with which they are incompatible occur, this tension occurs. The dissonance, and the unpleasant aftertaste it leaves, will lead people to try to restore coherence. Although the reduction of dissonance can occur in different ways, the result is usually a change in attitudes.

An example of how dissonance relates to cognitive dissonance is as follows. Let's say that a person is considered good. Let's imagine that this person participates in the Milgram experiment. Our person considers that it is good to obey authority, and she wants to continue considering herself like this. Therefore, this person will obey the researcher and give stronger shocks each time the other participant fails in the answers. If he did not obey, the dissonance would appear.

She will not consider the option of disobeying because she does not want to distance herself from the attributes that distinguish a good person for her. It is true that she also considers that it is good not to torture others with downloads, but at first, these downloads are slight. So, between the two attributes, at first, she chooses to obey the investigator.

On the other hand, as downloads rise, the power of the two opposing behaviors is also balanced.

In defense of the label that she wants to keep for herself (that of a good person), so that dissonance will also grow.

When this occurs, the person applying the downloads stops managing them or continues. In the first case, to safeguard your image against the fact of having disobeyed, your mind is likely to begin to question that authority. In the second case, for the same purpose, the person can become convinced that the downloads do not cause as much damage as it seems. And the person who receives them is pretending or that they are good for them since, according to the researcher (authority), they improve their learning.

In any case, by opting for one of the two options, your mind will attack the other, so that the person who administers the downloads can continue to consider themselves a good person.

The role of emotions

Until now, we have talked, above all, about changes in attitudes, thoughts, and behaviors, but there is another factor of great importance, emotions. Despite the general idea that emotions follow one path while logical reasoning follows another, this is a fallacy.

According to Damasio (1994), emotions always influence reasoning, even if it is logical. Furthermore, if emotions did not influence, the decisions we would make would not be socially accepted. Think, for example, of psychopaths who do not regulate emotions and fail to empathize. Their decisions are for their benefit, but they leave other people aside.

Therefore, one form of social influence, which is transversal to the other previously explained forms, consists of appealing to emotions. Manipulating emotions is considered, from logic, a fallacy since instead of giving logical reasoning, attempts are made to change emotions so that this results in a change in attitudes. This will especially affect those people who let their emotions greatly influence their reasoning processes.

In conclusion, we could say that it is very easy to influence others, but, in turn, it is no less difficult to be influenced. As we have seen, social groups and people in authority are going to influence us a lot. The best way to manage these influences is to know the mechanisms of influence and try to be aware of when they occur.

CHAPTER 13

THE 4 PERSONALITY TYPES

A group of American researchers suggest that there are four personality types based on five personality traits.

Throughout the history of psychology, various authors have developed different theories of personality, including different personality types. Recently, a group of researchers from the University of the Northwest, in Evanston, Illinois (USA), have carried out an exhaustive analysis of data, the results of which challenge established paradigms in psychology. Martin Gerlach led the study.

Social psychologists question whether personality types exist. Traits are another matter. Personality traits "can be measured consistently across ages, across cultures," said Amaral, co-author of the study, professor of chemical and biological engineering at the McCormick School of Engineering at Northwestern University.

Researchers have reviewed data from more than 1.5 million respondents and found that there are at least four distinct groups of personality types: average, reserved, self-centered, and role model. These four personality types are based on five basic personality traits: neuroticism, extraversion, openness, kindness, and conscience. The new study has been published by the journal Nature Human Behavior.

A still-controversial concept in psychology

William Revelle, professor of psychology at the Weinberg College of Arts and Sciences and lead author of the study, explains that "people have tried to classify personality types since the time of Hippocrates, but previous scientific literature has found that this has not made sense." The data from this new research shows that "there are higher densities of certain personality types."

However, at first, Revelle was skeptical about the premise presented by the study. In psychology, the definition of personality types remains controversial, particularly as empirical support has been given to several classifications. Past attempts focused on small groups of research yielded mostly findings that could not be replicated.

"Forms of personality existed only in the literature of self-help, and had no place in scientific journals," says Amaral. "Because of this analysis, we conclude that this will change now."

Personality types: a new approach

The latest work combined an alternative statistical method with data from four questionnaires of more than 1.5 million respondents from around the world. This consisted of 120 and 300 items collected from John Johnson's IPIP-NEO, respectively, the "myPersonality" project and the data sets from the evidence of the BBC's great personality.

The questionnaires, developed by the research community for decades, have between 44 and 300 questions. People voluntarily respond to online questionnaires, attracted by the opportunity to receive comments about their personality.

From this large set of data, the team of researchers identified the five traits that are perhaps most widely accepted: neuroticism, extraversion, openness, kindness, and awareness. After developing new algorithms, four personality groups or types emerged:

- **Average rate.** Normal people are high in neuroticism and extraversion and low in transparency. According to the researchers, women are more likely to belong to the average type.

- **Reserved type.** The reserved type is emotionally stable, as well as not very neurotic. Those who belong to this group are not particularly extraverted, which does not mean that their treatment is pleasant.

- **Model to follow.** People belonging to the Role Model personality type have a low score in neuroticism and a high score in all other traits. The probability that someone is a role model increases dramatically with age. According to the researchers, these are trustworthy people and open to new ideas, and they are good people to be in charge of things. They also say that women are more likely to belong to this group.

- **Self-centered people.** Self-centered people score high in extraversion and are below average in openness, kindness, and conscience. There is a very drastic decline in the number of egocentric forms in both females and males as people age.

Personality changes throughout life

The researchers explain that as people mature, their personality settings change. For example, older people tend to be less neurotic, though more aware and personable than people under the age of 20.

"When we look at large population groups, it is clear that there are trends, and that these trends can also change over time, " Amaral said.

CHAPTER 14

THE SECRETS OF SUBLIMINAL PSYCHOLOGY

The subliminal is that which is below the threshold of consciousness. When the term is applied to a stimulus, it refers to the fact that it is not perceived consciously, but it still influences behavior.

A subliminal message is designed for the recipient to receive on an unconscious level. It may be, for example, an image that is transmitted so briefly that consciousness does not notice it, but it is etched in memory.

It is said that subliminal content is used by some advertising, although the transmission of such messages usually in advertising is punishable by law. With subliminal advertising, it is possible to present a product or service to the consumer so that the consumer feels like acquiring it without knowing the authentic reasons that lead to this.

For example, there are those who say that the Coca-Cola bottle has the shape of a woman's silhouette, to subliminally "conquer" those who feel sexual attraction to the female gender.

It should be remembered that subliminal publicity is not associated with advertisements in connection with social groups, a practice that is legally legitimate, and does nothing unconscious. An example of associative advertising is tobacco commercials, which often show smokers as sensual and interesting subjects, happy and proud of their lives. They show no trace of the fundamental reasons that lead a person to smoke: stress, personal dissatisfaction, shyness, and insecurity, among others. In this way, the consumer can interpret that if he smokes, he will obtain, for example, success on the sentimental level.

Subliminal positive affirmations

Finally, we can mention positive subliminal affirmations, which are phrases that are recorded so that the receiver listens to them repeatedly, and their unconscious assimilates the information. Positive subliminal affirmations are used to quit smoking or eliminate phobias, for example.

Subliminal tools in entertainment

Derren Brown is a very famous British mentalist and illusionist in his land, who, in recent years, has made all kinds of shows on theater and television to try to convince his viewers of the truth of his power. Their tricks usually have a common denominator: making the participant discover a secret on their own, without even knowing how they did it.

In 2009, a special that he made on English television was very popular, through which he tried to generate a kind of collective hypnosis, making his viewers believe that they were going to connect in a large energy network ... or lie. During the minutes before the moment long-awaited by millions of English people tired of the crude and boring reality, Derren explained that it would be necessary to sit in a comfortable position. They would need to be watching the television closely for a few seconds, after which, he assured, the entire public he would share the feeling of not being able to get up from the seat no matter how hard he tried.

He also warned that one could suffer from profound exhaustion and even dizziness so that those who were not willing to provoke this state chose to stay out of the experiment. Fortunately for the unbelievers, but unfortunately for the billionaire man of the show, the broadcast of the program on the Internet exposed the trick that did affect viewers: a series of unpleasant and grim images were broadcast for very short periods throughout the alleged hypnosis, without being seen on a conscious level.

Subliminal Persuasion

Subliminal programming has always had some enigmatic pictures in it. While it has become more popular lately, it is still kept by many people at an arm's length. Perhaps they are not completely ready to believe in its efficacy, or they are rather apprehensive about using it, and what they might do with their lives.

But subliminal persuasion is not some hidden hocus pocus, although it is very successful and strong. It all revolves around the subconscious mind's energy. In using subliminal manipulation, you are making full use of your mind's unbounded capabilities. And this ability is the product of our mind's inherent strength. There is nothing wrong with using it to make our lives easier. It is only natural for us to learn how it functions and use it to live life to its full potential.

And once you have opened yourself to this influence, you can take advantage of subliminal persuasion. It will help to make the conditions more favorable. Below are The Secrets of Subliminal Psychology to achieving meaningful results in daily circumstances.

1. **Psychology in reverse.**

    Reverse psychology is one of the subliminal persuasion techniques, which is the easiest and most effective. Unfortunately, it is being used by a lot of people now, and it has become quite a popular term. People have started using it too overtly, and that has weakened its usefulness because many people know reverse psychology automatically when they see it. Yet that does not mean that when you have any persuading to do, you should take it out.

    Reverse psychology makes use of the power of subliminal persuasion, and you can always rely on its persuasive ability. And the trick is to use it subtly. If you use the same scripts on reverse psychology, tell them in a way that hides the fact that you are using a strategy of persuasion.

Nevertheless, it can produce unexpected results when used correctly.

2. **Bring coincidences together.**

A coincidence is another important instrument that can be used for subliminal persuasion. Most people no longer necessarily believe in coincidences, but others still do. Then there are also a lot of people who think that they are not believers but are often persuaded when they find a very shocking one. It can still be very convincing to see correlations between things and find sense in them.

And if you want to convince anyone to do so, you could use coincidences. The problem is, how is that possible? You can't make coincidences happen after all; otherwise, they'll no longer be coincidences. Okay, by designing and organizing situations and events, you can make coincidences appear to happen, but subtly, so as not to show that they are occurring by design.

3. **Enlist senses of the people.**

Speech can be a straightforward weapon of persuasion, but if you want to persevere a little more subtly, why don't you target the other senses? Place an idea in someone's mind, for example, use a perfume that will remind the person of something relevant to what you want.

4. **Calling a person by his first name.**

   Did you know that the simple act of calling someone by the first name is already a powerful technique of subliminal persuasion? There is no conclusive justification as to why this works, but it does. Others claim to do so helps make requests more intimate, so he or she feels more committed and becomes more likely to act on them.

Subliminal Psychology in An Intimate Relationship

Relationships require a lot of time; the work involved in sustaining a relationship will, in reality, never end. Unfortunately, there are a lot of factors outside our control that relationships often seem to take a backseat in life. This, and because these relationships are by nature highly reactive, they are easily weakened over time. But some of the strongest marriages buckle down under life's stresses and demands.

It is natural to go through rough patches in a relationship. But if issues aren't immediately fixed, they begin to pile up and accumulate. There comes a make or break point in most relationships. When you're on the verge of a broken relationship, turning it around isn't too late.

1. **Un-Pollute the Mind and Connection.**

   It can still save all troubled relationships. The

reason a lot of people settle for going their separate ways is that they don't know how to solve the issues that arise in the relationship correctly.

But the fact is, the reasons you first joined the relationship are still there. Most likely, they just got lost under all the stresses, expectations, environmental factors, negative talk and understanding of relationships in general, and so forth. Add to that all the unresolved problems that trigger negative emotions like mistrust, fear, doubt, and suppressed anger.

All you have to do to save a relationship is to unravel the reasons and strengthen them again. Remember why you were interested in the relationship and see if those reasons still hold. If they do, it's all just a matter of removing all the relationship-damaging layers accumulated that pollute the relationship.

How will you take these off?

2. **Attract Positive Improvements as Substitution.**

Now that all those undermining layers are gone, you have plenty of room in your relationship for positive changes. Imagining the kind of relationship you want to have invites an instant positive change in your relationship. Focus your mind on the positive changes in the relationship you want to see happen. Invite these thoughts and improvements by the use of strong subliminal messages into actualization.

Subliminal messages have the power to control your conduct and acts. And if you fill your mind with them, you'll certainly see changes happening.

And what changes will subliminal messages and couple self-help welcome into your revived relationship?

- Help you overcome frustrating feelings
- Allow you to step forward and leave your old baggage behind
- Help you settle disagreements and come up with mutually beneficial solutions
- Help you see and embrace personality differences
- Shape a common vision
- Deepen confidence
- Make a relationship

It will not be sufficient to save a relationship cycle without plans for future problems that are sure to come. And if after a while you don't want to end up in the same make or break point again, you've got to learn how to manage the relationship properly.

It does not take an expert to fix issues with the partnership. You don't need to go straight to ask a counselor. There are plenty of tips on self-help relationships, and you can work out things together and as one.

CHAPTER 15

HOW TO USE DARK PSYCHOLOGY IN SEDUCTION

The reason seduction is a mind game is that most people have deep psychological needs that are not satisfied. You can seduce your target if you find out the needs of the other person and put yourself in such a way that you can suggest that you can satisfy them. The explanation behind this is that we're driven more than anything by our feelings, given what we'd like to believe. If there is a conflict between reason and heart inside our-selves, the heart always wins. Read on and learn how to use these timeless seduction rules.

You must stand for something, and you must embody something. You can tailor that to your target e.g., if they like the quiet, sensitive, saintly but secretly sexually threatening type, you can become that. Be mysterious. Always, even after a relationship begins, maintain the mystery, keep some corners dark. Display a blank, mysterious face onto which people can project their fantasies. People are dying to be allowed to fantasize about you—do not spoil this golden opportunity by overexposing yourself. Familiarity is the death of seduction. Never declare your feelings for your target. Never say, 'I love you.' Instead, mention your feelings. Love not stated speaks volumes. Be ambiguous, hard to figure out.

Low self-esteem is repellent. Don't put yourself down and don't show weakness. People treat you as you treat yourself, and if they sense weakness, they pounce on it. What is natural to your character is inherently seductive. Appearing to be secure is sexy. However, displaying overt strength and power is not. Learn to play up your natural weaknesses and flaws after the person has known you for a while. Having an air of sadness is seductive, especially if that sadness appears to be spiritual in origin and not merely a product of a depressed mood. Depth and complexity draw people in. Anything that cannot be understood is seductive. Always be positive. Take a step back, be distant, narcissistic. Never appear jealous but make people jealous by hinting that you may not be that interested in them.

To appear charismatic, keep the source of your charisma secret. Charisma springs from and plays on repressed sexuality. Because their lack of freedom oppresses most people, they are drawn by people who appear to be more free and fluid. Dandies are subtle and never try hard to gain attention—small touches produce the effect they create. At all costs, you must embody something, anything to avoid the taint of familiarity and commonness. Do not allow yourself to be easily manipulated—you appear less attractive that way—attractive traits: being a leader, knowledgeable in many subjects, good conversationalist, not appearing needy. Appear to be desireless. Appear to be excellent. Do not flirt blatantly—send mixed signals

CHAPTER 16

GAMES THEORY

Have you noticed that an opponent has a particular mania, for example, that he tends to joke when he has an excellent hand but that he remains silent when he bluffs? This is very good, psychology is a formidable weapon in poker, and this observation could be useful for you, provided you know how to use it.

When you have noticed, thanks to an opponent's tell, a defect in his game, you must be patient. In poker, the strokes follow each other but are not alike, and you may need to play a hundred hands with this opponent before the situation happens again. Even if it does happen again, you have to be in a position to win the pot.

If you recognize a tell from a player that he is bluffing, but you do not have enough play to beat a bluff, do not pay even if you know full well that your opponent is cheekily lying. The goal of poker is not to be right but to make money!

... And use it with discretion.

It is very important to be discreet when using an opponent's tell. On the one hand, so that he does not notice it, and on the other hand, so that the other players of the table do not notice it. Not see either, so there is no point in claiming on all the rooftops that you paid a bluff because your opponent's right hand was shaking, even if they are accusing you of having played badly.

The most important thing in poker is to get the most out of the shots and keep your weapons and their secret benefits as long as possible. The more people around the table were trying to exploit a tell, the less it will earn you money.

Professional players know how to handle tells and push psychology even further, they can lead you to believe that they make mistakes only to surprise you when you think you can exploit them. Beware of tells that are too big to be true.

Tells like deception

As you can guess above, even if you are not good at psychology or observation and you do not spot the tells of your opponents, you can still use this facet of poker. Lots of professional players only play with pot odds and the value of their hands, without the tells, especially when they come from the internet world, so you don't have to worry.

Manipulate your opponents by making them believe you have a major mistake, and we can see this action to a lesser degree in online poker with players who "tank" (think for a long time) before jumping into it all in. Whether they played the watch (or, on the contrary, they behaved almost instantly) remains to be seen to make you think they're bluffing or, because they've got an excellent deck.

CONCLUSION

It is time to conclude from these findings that social norms, rules, and values are "not natural" for human beings, and that society frequently imposes group action based on what the powerful want over the powerless. Because survival mentality is our norm, what society is attempting to do is to regulate the wild beast in every human being. This is done by educating them from an early age to follow the control group's laws, rules, and morality, typically the wealthy, who dominate our governments and institutions. Therefore, should we denounce those who feel that society does not give them a reasonable deal-who will, in turn, take what they need to survive in an often hostile world where privilege depends on your education, family, or wealth? Will psychology itself have to come out of the closet and accept that normal human conduct is in contrast to strict structures and regulations? That people hate society, but they experience some helplessness in trying to survive among the sheep because they are powerless against those who regulate the law-making and morality? Is it any wonder that sometimes an alone person takes it into their own hands to change society or their own life to live a freer self-controlled existence away from the rigors of societies? Which all inevitably crumble and reinvent themselves as the newly rich and the powerful take control once again? Over the last century, we saw China turning itself from an empire dominated by depots into a military dictatorship controlled by the rich and powerful into a communist look of the 1950s in which Communism will decide a decent life for all.

The China of today as a capitalist democratic state is based on a political party that decides the lives of the poor people, who fought for it. Will there be another revolution in China in the future? It seems doubtful at the moment, given the turmoil in many parts of China by minorities unable to comply with the central rule. Could not all powers see their downfall! Can psychology then answer this problem of human actions as a basic survival mechanism because, in reality, human beings are inherently aggressive, cruel, and superior over those who are weaker than themselves? In mental institutions, psychiatry is also seen as the agents of social order—if you disagree with society and its laws. Then you must be insane—thus you should be arrested and regulated for the health and good of all.

On the other hand, psychology is seen as the therapeutic component of mental wellbeing, where we help those who are out of step with culture find their position and fit back into what is considered common behavior for that group. What is the answer to those who revolt against the society in which they live and want a better way of life out of the control of the powerful and the right to live a life they want as their own? And are we waiting for the films to come true? The tragedy that threatens all humans and a return to the life of a dog eat dog called survival—the real social norm!

www.ingramcontent.com/pod-product-compliance
Lightning Source LLC
Chambersburg PA
CBHW070900080526
44589CB00013B/1144